May this supreme, peerless teaching,

The precious treasure of the Victorious Ones

Spread and extend throughout the world,

Like the sun shining in the sky.

GOLDEN ROSARY EDITIONS

*comprise oral teachings by
Khenchen Thrangu Rinpoche on the great
lineage masters of the Kagyu tradition.*

*They are reproduced through
the inspiration of H.H. Karmapa,
the blessing of Khenchen Thrangu Rinpoche,
and the guidance of Venerable Lama Karma Shedrup.*

*These editions are dedicated
to their long life and prosperity.*

Zhyisil Chokyi Ghatsal Trust
Publications

The Life *of* Tilopa
&
The Ganges Mahamudra

by
Khabje Khenchen
Thrangu Rinpoche

Copyright © 2002 Namo Buddha Publications &
Zhyisil Chokyi Ghatsal Publications.

All rights reserved. No part of this book, either text or art, may be reproduced in any form, electronic or otherwise, without written permission form Thrangu Rinpoche or Namo Buddha Publications.

ISBN Number: 1-877294-22-5

This publication is a joint venture between:

Namo Buddha Publications
P. O. Box 1083, Crestone,
CO 81131, USA
Email: cjohnson@ix.netcom.com
Thrangu Rinpoche's web site: www.rinpoche.com
and

Zhyisil Chokyi Ghatsal Trust Publications
PO Box 6259 Wellesley Street,
Auckland, New Zealand
Email: inquiries@greatliberation.org
www.greatliberation.org

Acknowledgments

We would like to thank Jerry Morrell for translating the teachings given in Boulder and Jules Levinson for translating the teachings given in Nepal, Gaby Hollmann for transcribing and editing the Boulder and Nepal teachings, and to Lama Yeshe Gyamtso for his translation of the root text and translation of some of the Nepal teachings.

Notes

Technical words are italicized the first time that they appear to alert the reader that their definition can be found in the Glossary of Terms. The Tibetan words are given as they are pronounced, not spelled in Tibetan. We use B.C.E. (Before Current Era) for B.C. and C.E. (Current Era) for A.D.

Table of Contents

Foreword — xi
Biography of Thrangu Rinpoche — xiii
Preface — xv

PART I: THE LIFE OF TILOPA

Chap. 1 — An Introduction to the Spiritual Biography — 1

2 — Tilopa's Childhood — 5

3 — Tilopa Renounces Samsara and Meets his Teachers — 9

4 — Tilopa Receives Secret Instructions — 19

5 — Tilopa Gains Eight Pupils — 25

PART II: THE GANGES MAHAMUDRA

The Root Text 33

Chap. 6 *Introduction to Ganges Mahamudra* 43
  The Name of the Text
  The Homage
  A Brief Explanation of the Text

7 *The View of Mahamudra* 49
  A Detailed Explanation of the Text
  The View of Mahamudra in Six Points
  - Space as an Example of the Absence of Solidity
  - Space as an Example of When Mahamudra is Practiced
  - Mist Illustrating the Way Thoughts Dissolve
  - Space as an Example of Changelessness
  - Sunlight as Mind Being Empty and Also Luminosity
  - The Inexpressibility of the Mind's Nature

8 *The Conduct of Mahamudra* 67
  The Conduct of Actual Meditation
  Post-Meditation Conduct

9 *The Meditation of Mahamudra* 77

10 *The Samaya of Mahamudra* 83

11 *The Benefits of Practicing Mahamudra* 89

12 The Defects of Not Practicing Mahamudra — 93

13 How to Practice Mahamudra — 97
The Manner of Practicing Mahamudra
How to Engage in the Preliminaries
- How to Rely Correctly on a Guru and Gain a Correct Ascertainment
- The Ground, Path, and Fruition
- How to Abandon Distraction and Rely Upon Isolation
- The Benefits of Meditation upon Mahamudra

14 The Main Practice of Mahamudra — 117
How to Engage in the Main Body of Practice
- The Practice for Those of Highest Faculties
- A Restatement of the View, Meditation, Conduct and Fruition from a Resultant Point of View
- The Practice for Those of Medium or Lesser Faculties
- The Result of the Practice of Mahamudra

Dedication and Aspiration
The Colophon

Notes — 139
Glossary of Terms — 149
Index — 177

Ven. Lama Karma Shedrup Cho Gyi Senge Kartung

Foreword

The Golden Rosary Editions contain the spiritual biographies and teachings of the glorious Kagyupa lineage. The term "Golden Rosary" refers to this lineage of realized masters who have transmitted unbroken the profound Mahamudra teachings of the Lord Buddha to the present day. What makes these teachings so profound is that they contain instructions and practices which enable one to accomplish enlightenment in one lifetime.

One of the tremendous blessings of the Kagyu lineage is the diversity of lifestyles manifested by the lineage masters, showing that whatever our circumstances or lifestyle, we can practice these teachings and accomplish enlightenment. For example, Tilopa accomplished enlightenment while working as a menial labourer grounding sesame seeds. Others like Marpa were businessmen and had families. Marpa's student Milarepa was an ascetic who spent his life practicing in isolated caves, and one of his students, Gampopa, was a monk. Yet what they all had in common was that through practicing Mahamudra they all accomplished enlightenment. All this shows the great variety and power of the methods of Vajrayana for transforming one's mind through whatever circumstances. So similarly, if we practice Mahamudra with great diligence and effort we can achieve the fruition in one lifetime.

Therefore to read these spiritual biographies of the Kagyu lineage masters is a great inspiration to enter the path and they also provide encouragement and inspiration to continue when circumstances become difficult. In particular it is of great blessing to receive these teachings from Khenchen Thrangu Rinpoche, a master of great wisdom and compassion. Because he has directly realised Mahamudra and is a holder of this lineage he can transmit not only the words but the meaning.

So, I encourage all students to read these spiritual biographies and pray that it will inspire you to fulfil all the aspirations of the lineage masters. And may this merit cause the life and teachings of the great masters to flourish and remain for many aeons benefiting limitless sentient beings.

Zhyisil Chokyi Ghatsal Trust
3/1 Franklin Rd, Ponsonby
Auckland, NZ

Biography of Thrangu Rinpoche (b. 1933)

The lineage of the Thrangu Rinpoche incarnations began in the fifteenth century when the Seventh Karmapa, Chodrak Gyatso visited the region of Thrangu in Tibet. At this time His Holiness Karmapa established Thrangu Monastery and enthroned Sherap Gyaltsen as the first Thrangu Rinpoche, recognizing him as the re-established emanation of Shuwu Palgyi Senge, one of the twenty-five great siddha disciples of Guru Padmasambhava.

Khenchen Thrangu Rinpoche is the ninth incarnation of this lineage and was born in Kham, Tibet in 1933. When he was four, H.H. the Sixteenth Gyalwa Karmapa and Palpung Situ Rinpoche recognized him as the incarnation of Thrangu Tulku by prophesying the names of his parents and the place of his birth.

He entered Thrangu monastery and from the ages of seven to sixteen he studied reading, writing, grammar, poetry, and astrology, memorised ritual texts, and completed two preliminary retreats. At sixteen under the direction of Khenpo Lodro Rabsel he began the study of the three vehicles of Buddhism while staying in retreat.

At twenty-three he received full ordination from the Karmapa. When he was twenty-seven Rinpoche left Tibet for India at the time of the Communist invasion. He was called to Rumtek, Sikkim, where the Karmapa had his seat in exile. At thirty-five he took the geshe examination before 1500 monks at Buxador monastic refugee camp in Bengal India and was awarded the degree of Geshe Lharampa. On his return to Rumtek he was named Abbot of Rumtek monastery and the Nalanda Institute for Higher Buddhist studies at Rumtek. He has been the personal teacher of the four principal Karma Kagyu tulkus: Shamar Rinpoche, Situ Rinpoche, Jamgon Kongtrul Rinpoche and Gyaltsab Rinpoche.

Thrangu Rinpoche has travelled extensively throughout Europe, the Far East and the USA. He is the abbot of Gampo Abbey, Nova Scotia, and of Thrangu House, Oxford, in the UK. In 1984 he spent several months in Tibet where he ordained over 100 monks and nuns and visited several monasteries. He has also founded Thrangu Tashi Choling monastery in Boudhnath; a retreat centre and college at Namo Buddha east of the Katmandu Valley, and has established a school in Boudhnath for the general education of lay children and young monks. He also built Tara Abbey in Katmandu. In October of 1999 he consecrated the college at Sarnath which will accept students from the different traditions of Buddhism and will be open to western students as well.

Thrangu Rinpoche, a recognised master of Mahamudra meditation has given teachings in over 25 countries. He is especially known for taking complex teachings and making them accessible to western students.

More recently, because of his vast knowledge of the Dharma, he was appointed by His Holiness the Dalai Lama to be the personal tutor for the Seventeenth Karmapa Urgyen Trinley Dorje.

Preface

The Buddhist teachings began with the life of the Buddha four centuries before our era. After the passing away of the Buddha there has been the continual challenge of preserving these teachings. In about the first century of our era, the Theravada teachings were preserved by taking them to Sri Lanka and having them committed to writing there. These and the Mahayana teachings of Northern India were carried on in the great monastic monasteries by thousands of practicing students until the Moslem invasions of India beginning in the ninth century C.E. Fortunately, a few very brave individuals from China and Tibet ventured down to India and carried back these Buddhist manuscripts. Just before the destruction of all the northern Buddhist monasteries – a dedicated Tibetan (Marpa Lotswa) traveled for years to India and was able to find Naropa – a scholar who had left the University of Nalanda to seek enlightenment in the forest by studying under the great mahasiddha Tilopa. This connection brought a special lineage of Vajrayana teachings to Tibet and these were preserved and practiced, passing from guru to student to this very day.

These teachings were passed down through the Kagyu lineage – one of the major lineages of Buddhism in Tibet – and this book is the first biography of these lineage holders.

In 1988 the Nalanda Translation Committee in the United States asked Thrangu Rinpoche to give teachings on Tilopa because they were translating a biography on him. Thrangu Rinpoche gave these teachings at Karma Dzong in Boulder, Colorado on October, 1988 with Jerry Morrell translating. Namo Buddha Publications was fortunate to receive a copy of these teachings and this text was transcribed and edited by Gaby Hollmann in Munich, 1990.

Thrangu Rinpoche also gave teachings on Tilopa in Nepal to the Namo Buddha Seminar in January of 1991 while the seminar was doing a pilgrimage to Lumbini, the birthplace of the Buddha. Since Rinpoche emphasized certain points in one set of teachings and other points in the other, these two teachings were combined to give the present text. We have also included some notes to help clarify and expand these points.

The text which Thrangu Rinpoche used for his teachings on Tilopa was the Pekar Chojung from Pema Karpo's *The History of the Dharma*.

Clark Johnson, Ph. D.
Namo Buddha Publications

PART I

The Life of Tilopa

Master Tilopa[1] and Vajradhara

1

Introduction to the Spiritual Biography

A spiritual biography of a great mahasiddha or any great lama is called a *namtar* in Tibetan which means a *hagiography* or story of realization. A spiritual biography is not just a biography which discusses when and where a person was born and other biographical details, but rather it is a story of the events that lead to the realization of the individual.

A namtar discusses how that individual began the practice of meditation, how he or she applied themselves to the *dharma*, what methods that person used to accomplish realization, and how this realization led to helping other beings. Since they are stories of complete liberation from all suffering, they are called a "namtar" with the syllable *nam* meaning "complete" and the syllable *tar* meaning "liberation."

These spiritual biographies have few references to more mundane things of a mahasiddha's life such as what kind of clothes were worn, or what kind of food was eaten, or where he or she went. The reason for this is that the main purpose of a spiritual biography is to show a student of Buddhism how to practice the dharma, and the results of practicing the dharma by using an example of a person who has actually accomplished *Buddhahood*.

Many people say that Tibetan stories and spiritual biographies present only the good deeds and qualities of an individual with all the bad deeds being left out. One Tibetan author, Amdor Ganden Chophel who wrote the *White Annals* makes the point that Tibetan stories and biographies don't present the complete truth and gloss over some of the faults of lamas. There is some truth in this, but the purpose of a namtar is for the student to discover what the practice of dharma is actually like, what meditation is like, and to learn how love and compassion are expressed by the great practitioners. So the purpose of a namtar is to inspire the student and this is why they present all the marvelous qualities of the lamas and leave out the negative ones.

Western scholars ask, "How can these biographies be taken seriously? They don't provide a birth date, the actual place names, and other details of the mahasiddha's life." This is true, but why does one need to know when these people lived? Perhaps Tilopa lived in the fifth century, perhaps in the seventh century. But who actually cares? Tilopa was not an ordinary human being anyway. We remember the great kindness and great efforts of Tilopa and Naropa who made the teachings of *Mahamudra* and the *Six Yogas of Naropa*[2] available to all of those in Tibet, and now to students all over the whole world.

The Buddha gave numerous teachings of the *sutras* and of the *tantras* which make up the *84,000 classes of dharma*. He taught the entire path of dharma in an extremely vast way. If we, however, try to study all the sutras and tantras, it would be very difficult to extract their pith instructions and find out how to actually travel on the path. The great mahasiddha Tilopa, however, extracted the very essence of these vast teachings of the sutras and tantras and explained exactly how we develop this practice. An analogy is that if we go into a forest in the high mountains, we may know that the forest is full of medicine. However, this knowledge is useless unless we also know which particular plant is a medicinal plant and which particular illness the plant can be used for.

Introduction to the Spiritual Biography

Tilopa and Chakrasamvara

Tilopa (988-1069 C.E.) was an emanation of *Chakrasamvara*.[3] He practiced the dharma perfectly and obtained complete *enlightenment*. Now, Tilopa was not able to see the supreme *nirmanakaya* emanation of the Buddha Shakyamuni[4] who passed away many centuries before. However, the *dharmakaya* is replete with the unbelievable power of compassion which manifests continuously to all sentient beings. This dharmakaya aspect as well as the compassion aspect of the *sambhogakaya* goes on for the benefit of all sentient beings. Tilopa had direct experience of this dharmakaya aspect and received all the pith instructions of practice directly from the Buddha *Vajradhara*.[5]

Because of the *obscurations* and negative accumulations of sentient beings they are not able to perceive the form of Chakrasamvara directly. So Chakrasamvara emanates as an impure being, an ordinary manifestation being born among humans so he is visible to human beings who need to be taught about how to gain liberation. Without any doubt Tilopa was an emanation of Chakrasamvara.[6] If Chakrasamvara were to emanate in the human realm without relying on a particular teacher, doing a particular practice, or following any particular tradition then people would think, "Well, this is a being from somewhere else and it isn't possible for me to be like him in any way." They simply would not practice. So Chakrasamvara manifested as an ordinary being who then received all the practice instructions and who then practiced these instructions, and finally accomplished enlightenment. This is how emanations of Chakrasamvara manifest to help sentient beings.

In India the great mahasiddha Tilopa took up the practice of dharma and achieved the ultimate results [enlightenment]. He brought the pith instructions of Mahamudra and the Six Yogas of Naropa to our world. These teachings went directly from him to Naropa, and were then carried to Tibet by Marpa and flourished widely there. Even today, a thousand years later, these very same teachings are spreading throughout the world and to Western countries. This is a sign of the great wisdom, compassion, and power of the mahasiddha Tilopa.

The great translator Marpa received mainly the transmission of Mahamudra meditation and the Six Yogas of Naropa from Tilopa's student Naropa. He received these in the form of the Hevajra tantra and more specifically in the Chakrasamvara tantra. In the *mandala* of Chakrasamvara Marpa received the essence of *skilful means* (Skt. *upaya*) as Chakrasamvara and the essence of wisdom (Skt. *prajna*) as Vajrayogini. The mandala of the union of skilful means and wisdom is the basis of the Chakrasamvara tantra. When we visualize ourself as Hevajra or Chakrasamvara in these tantras, we are engaging in the *creation stage* of meditation. The meditation on the Six Yogas of Naropa is the *completion stage* of the Chakrasamvara tantra.

2

Tilopa's Childhood

Tilopa was born in eastern India in 988 C.E. When Tilopa was a young boy, he had the rather special qualities of being extremely compassionate, kind, and loving. He was a cowherd and played in the forest without a care. At the time, the great Nagarjuna[7] was out walking in that part of India. He had the insight that somewhere in this region was an individual who was an ideal vessel to receive the *Vajrayana* teachings. Pondering this he proceeded in the direction between the town and the river where Tilopa was taking care of the water buffaloes. Nagarjuna wanted to cross the river and pretended not to know where to ford the river. He went to a point with rapids and high waves and pretended that he was going to walk into the raging river. Tilopa came running up to him and said to him, "I will help you by carrying you across. There is no need for you to be afraid or trouble yourself." Nagarjuna saw instantly that this child had great qualities for developing intense devotion and compassion and that he had the capacity for extreme courage and diligence. He allowed the boy to carry him into the river. Although Tilopa was young and Nagarjuna was an adult, by his miraculous power Nagarjuna made his body so light that the boy could carry him quite easily.

Tilopa carried him into the river and when they got to the middle of the river, Nagarjuna using his miraculous powers made the river rise very high. The raging torrent almost carried the boy away so that he was about to disappear beneath the waves. The young Tilopa didn't think, "Oh, I've made a mistake. We shouldn't have tried this," but rather developed a firm determination to get to the other side and wasn't afraid at all.

Nagarjuna tested him even further and exclaimed, "All is lost. We are done for. There is nothing to grab onto. We will never get to the other side of the river." But Tilopa developed even greater determination and said to Nagarjuna, "Just hold on tight to my neck and I'll get you to the other side. Don't worry. We are going to do this." So, Nagarjuna saw he had great courage and potential and was indeed a fit vessel for all the dharma teachings.

On another occasion Nagarjuna was again traveling in the neighborhood and came upon the scene of the young Tilopa playing that he was a king. He was sitting at the bottom of a tree with a couple of girls pretending to be his queens; four little children pretending to be his inner court, other children pretending to be the outer court, and twenty-five children acting as his subjects. Seeing this, Nagarjuna came up to them smiling. The young Tilopa jumped up and prostrated to Nagarjuna and said, "How are you? Did you have a hard time on your journey?" Nagarjuna said, "I have the means by which you can become a king." The young Tilopa responded, "Oh, please tell me the means. You must!" Nagarjuna spent seven days consecrating a special treasure vase. He wrote down the name of the king, the names of the queens, what kinds of ministers he would require, what kind of wealth and riches would be needed by the kingdom on a piece of paper and put it into the treasure vase. Then he gave it to Tilopa and said, "Say, 'I will be king' three times into this vase." Tilopa took the vase, put it to his mouth, and shouted inside it, "I will be king" three times.

It so happened that the king of the region suddenly became totally exasperated with his kingdom and decided he must give it up and go somewhere else. This was due to the great blessings and power of Nagarjuna and the magic treasure vase. Furthermore, this thought came to the king without anyone knowing about it. He dressed himself as an ordinary person and just left.

Tilopa's Childhood

This kingdom also had a most extraordinary elephant who had clairvoyant powers and would predict events in the kingdom. For instance, if there were any threats from enemies, the elephant would plow up the earth and toss it around. When a plague of some kind would threaten the kingdom, the elephant would cry and shed many tears. When good things happened in the kingdom, the elephant would rush into the local park and pull up the flowers and throw them all around. This elephant was also responsible for determining the future king. The elephant would take a crowning vase by picking it up with its trunk and place it on the head of the person who was to be the next king.

Not many people had noticed that their king had vanished. One day the elephant went to the vase he used to crown the next king with, picked it up, and began marching out of the palace towards the forest where young Tilopa was still playing his game of royal court. All the ministers and people ran behind the elephant, muttering to each other, "What's going on? Either the king is dying or our kingdom is finished." They followed the elephant to the group of children and the elephant placed the vase on top of Tilopa's head. Because the people of the kingdom believed completely in the elephant's choice, they took the young boy back into the palace of the kingdom and placed him upon the jeweled throne and made him their king.

At first the ministers and later all the subjects treated this boy-king with suspicion. They didn't obey his commands because they thought he was an ordinary person and his selection was actually some sort of mistake. So Tilopa prayed to Nagarjuna for guidance and Nagarjuna instructed Tilopa to mount his elephant, take a sword in one hand, and go out into the park, slap the trees in the park, and then tell them to go to war. Tilopa did this and when he slapped the trees, the trees turned into warriors, ready to go to war. When the subjects and ministers saw this, they thought, "Oh, this is a great king with incredible merit" and brought him back into the palace and accepted him as their true king.[8]

Another time the city of Tilopa's kingdom was approached by what looked like a horde of Persian merchants. They arrived on horseback dressed as ordinary merchants with big packs on the backs of their animals. The people and ministers of the kingdom saw them and didn't give them another thought. Actually they were Persian warriors disguised as merchants. When they stopped in front of the city, they got off their animals, undid their packs, put on all their armor and prepared to advance onto the city.

At this point everyone in the kingdom was terrified that there would be a great war and they would be destroyed. But Tilopa told them, "Don't be afraid. I'll take care of it." He went out in front of this horde of Persian warriors with his mantle, holding a stick with a globe on it and his sword. He stood before the approaching army and incredible light radiated from his mantle, dazzling all the Persian warriors so they couldn't look in his direction. Then Tilopa held up his sword and brandished it until many soldiers came flying out of the sword, scaring the Persian enemy completely away. After that the subjects and ministers were extremely happy with their king and celebrated and rejoiced.

So this concludes the second chapter on the childhood of Tilopa which tells how the poor cowherd became a king. This chapter shows us that one does not have to become poor and be an ascetic to practice the dharma.

3

Tilopa Renounces Samsara and Meets His Teachers

The outer action of any mahasiddha has three stages. The first stage is called the "all-good stage," the second is called the "stage of vanquishing behavior," and the third stage is called the "victorious in all directions behavior." A mahasiddha goes through these stages one by one. The first is called "all-good behavior" because the beginner must take up the practice of being extremely peaceful, calm, and carefully watch his or her actions by having extremely controlled and noble behavior. The beginner who engages in this behavior is able to advance along the path and then at a certain point, he or she must enter what is called the "vanquishing behavior" or *adul shug* in Tibetan. The syllable *adul* means "to vanquish" or "to subdue" and refers to one's *kleshas,* especially one's arrogance which is to be completely subdued by the practice. The syllable *shug* means "entering." So in this stage one actually submits oneself to conditions that may normally evoke disturbing consequences such as rage or desire. In the stage of all-good behavior the beginner avoids these situations, but in the vanquishing stage the meditator actually seeks them out. The meditator has to destroy arrogance, pride, and hatred by confronting them and throwing himself into situations that evoke the kind of response that allows him or her to work with these emotions. The third stage of "victorious in all directions behaviour" is the final expression of total fearlessness; it is a total lack of any inhibition about anything done. An example of this third kind of behavior would be fearlessly riding on the back of an incensed tigress and this stage is the final expression of one's realization.

So, we begin Vajrayana practice with the beginning level of "all-good behavior" and gradually work towards the final level of the practice of "victory in all directions." As beginners we must begin practicing the all-good behavior until true wisdom and realization arise and becomes a stable experiences for us. We cannot begin with the level of vanquishing behavior by doing such things as wearing bone ornaments and behaving like a mad man. These things are meditative practices for later on when we have gone through the various spiritual stages.

Therefore, at this point Tilopa began practicing the all-good behavior by maintaining his vows as a monk and studying very diligently. The story proceeds with Tilopa abandoning his life as a king and becoming a monk and entering the *Hinayana* path. This took place when, as a king, he developed great revulsion for *samsara*. Setting his own son up as royal heir, he left the kingdom and went to a cemetery called Somapuri where there was a temple erected over a spontaneously arisen form of the *Heruka*. At the time of Tilopa, this temple was considered holy by both Buddhists and non-Buddhists. Tilopa received full ordination as a monk or *bhikshu* and resided in Somapuri for a long time practicing diligently.

Tilopa Begins Vajrayana Meditation

However, Tilopa's meditation was interrupted by the sight of a very ugly hag who suddenly appeared in front of him. She had a bluish-gray complexion and yellow-colored hair. She appeared before him and distracted him by saying to Tilopa who was reading the *Prajnaparamita*, "Would you like to understand and directly experience the meaning of the Prajnaparamita?" At that moment Tilopa recognized that she was a real *dakini* and said to her, "Yes, I would like to really understand the meaning of this teaching. I want to understand it directly." The dakini then said to him, "Although what you have been studying is the pure and perfect teaching of the Buddha, it requires a great deal of hardship to actually attain fruition. You must practice virtuous behavior for very many lifetimes. This is a path with many obstacles and is difficult to travel and takes a great deal of time. The teachings I have to teach you are of the fruition tantra. With this practice you can attain fruition within one, three, or at the most seven lifetimes. This practice is very easy and there are few obstacles on this path. I am going to make you enter into the secret *Mantrayana*."[9]

The dakini transformed herself into the mandala of Chakrasamvara in the sky in front of him, giving Tilopa the pith instructions of the creation and completion stages of practice. In the creation stage one visualizes oneself as the deity and the practice is to destroy one's current neurotic fixation on gross and mundane phenomena. Since one can develop a fixation upon the deity itself, the dakini then taught Tilopa the pith instructions of the completion stage, which is basically the instruction on how to dissolve the immeasurable palace of the mandala into the deity, the deity into a seed syllable, and then the seed syllable into *emptiness*. With these two pith instructions, Tilopa attained a degree of realization and the dakini said, "Now throw out your bhikshu ordination and go about acting like a madman, practicing in secret so that nobody knows what you are doing," and then she vanished into the sky.

This dakini who bestowed these instructions and empowerments on Tilopa was called Karpo Sangmo. The reason for doing this vanquishing behavior of acting like a madman is that one has to test one's *samadhi* by enduring harsh conditions, such as being thrown into jail, being beaten up and robbed, and so on that this practice places one in. One combines the experience of these unfavorable conditions with the samadhi itself to experience the power of one's samadhi. This is a very powerful method to let go of one's neurotic conceptions.

This part of Tilopa's biography corrects the notion that people can accomplish enlightenment by themselves and that they don't need a teacher. Tilopa took a dakini as a teacher. That is why Marpa in his commentary on this part of Tilopa's life wrote, "He received the blessing from the great dakini Karpo Sangmo and she gave him the four empowerments."

The Four Empowerments

The first empowerment is called the "vase empowerment" which points out that the nature of one's five *skandhas* are the *five Buddha families*. There are five aspects of the vase empowerment: the vase empowerment of Akshobhya, the crown empowerment of Ratnasambhava, the vajra empowerment of Amitabha, the bell empowerment of Amoghasiddhi, and the name empowerment of Vairochana. Through these five stages of the vase empowerment, one recognizes the five skandhas as being the five Buddha families.

The second empowerment is called the "secret empowerment" and takes place through the actual experience of tasting and swallowing the healing nectar or *amrita* that is passed out in the empowerment. One swallows it and all the knots and blockages within the *subtle channels* (Skt. *nadis*) in the body and the life force (Skt. *prana*) are untied or liberated. With this one experiences an extremely even flow of the energy within the body. This is the empowerment of the energy flow, the channels, and the energy points (Skt. *bindu*) within the body and especially of the *mantra* itself.

The third empowerment is called the "knowledge and wisdom" empowerment in which one actually experiences *great bliss*. By experiencing great bliss one recognizes that it is inseparable from the nature of mind, that it is emptiness. So one attains an experience called "bliss-emptiness" which is called "approximate wisdom" or "an example of the actual wisdom of bliss-emptiness."

The fourth empowerment is called the "empowerment of the word" which explains the real nature of wisdom itself. These four empowerments are called "ripening empowerments" because when one receives these empowerments, one does not accomplish all the stages and so it is not that one never needs to practice any more. Rather, ripening empowerments should be taken as symbolic moments which eventually lead to fruition. So one feels that one has had the great fortune of receiving the empowerments and these will be connected with the full realization of these empowerments with further practice.

Tilopa Meets Matangi

After practicing the pith instructions for a long time, Tilopa found that he had reached a point where he could progress no further. He wanted to go to the south of India to find Nagarjuna once more. To do this he began walking through the jungle. In the jungle he saw a beautiful straw hut and wondered who was in there. Inside he found a *yogi*, who had no food, utensils, or clothes. Tilopa said to him, "What are you doing?" The yogi replied, "I am teaching dharma to the *gandharvas* (who are the spirits living off smell). I was told to teach the gandharvas by the great Nagarjuna himself. I have nothing here." Tilopa asked him, "Who feeds you?" He answered, "All the nature spirits and the deities of the forest bring me food." Tilopa then inquired, "What is your name?" and the yogi replied, "My name is Matangi" and told Tilopa that Nagarjuna was deceased and had entered *parinirvana*.

Tilopa asked Matangi to accept him as his student and Matangi accepted him. He then manifested the mandala of Guhyasamaja and gave him all the pith instructions of the creation and completion stages of this tantra. The Chakrasamvara tantra that Tilopa had received from the dakini Karpo Sangmo were instructions of the *mother tantra*. The instructions of Sangvadhupa from Matangi were of the *father tantra*. The basic difference between the mother tantra and father tantra is that the mother tantra emphasizes the completion stage which relies more on the emptiness aspect of the nature of mind. The father tantra emphasizes the creation stage and relies more on the *luminosity* (or clarity) aspect of the nature of mind. Based on Matangi's instructions, Tilopa completely achieved the stage of creation to the point where it was almost like seeing the *yidam* face to face. Tilopa had attained the wisdom arising from the creation stage and was now on the verge of completely accomplishing the completion stage. But Tilopa decided that he needed further instructions and left south India to go to northeast India where he sought out the teacher Nagpopa. From him Tilopa received the instructions and *empowerments* of the Chakrasamvara practice once again which he had already received from Karpo Sangmo. However, there are three lineages of Chakrasamvara with one coming from Luipa, the second from Nagpopa, and the third from Dribupa. This lineage of Chakrasamvara came from Nagpopa who became Tilopa's third teacher.

Tilopa received all the pith instructions of Nagpopa and became a fully accomplished practitioner in the completion stage. Even though he had completely accomplished these two stages of practice, he still hadn't realized the ultimate view. So he left that part of the country and went to the west of India where he encountered the great mahasiddha Lalapa. From Lalapa he received the pith instructions of Mahamudra, especially the "three heart sphere"[10] instructions and certain pith instructions. In this way Tilopa traveled to the four directions of India and became the disciple of the four great mahasiddhas: Matangi, Lalapa, Karpo Sangmo, and Nagpopa. He received all the mother tantra, the father tantra, and the Mahamudra instructions from them. He not only received these instructions, but practiced until he had fully mastered them.

Tilopa received further instructions from Matangi who said to him, "Now you must meditate continuously on the very essence of *suchness* and the nature of phenomena and mind. To do this you must find some kind of activity to engage in. Previously you were a king, so you have some vestige of class arrogance and this must be destroyed." Matangi ordered Tilopa to take the job of extracting oil from the sesame seeds by beating them, an occupation performed only by the lowest caste. Furthermore, Matangi told Tilopa that in the state of Bengal in eastern India there was a kingdom ruled by a very divine king, who was no ordinary king but an emanation of himself. This king had so blessed the land that whoever practiced meditation there would travel very rapidly on the path and attain exceedingly good results. Matangi also explained that in that kingdom there was a town called Harikila with a market

Tilopa Renounces Samsara and Meets His Teachers

place and a brothel. Tilopa must become a pimp and a servant to a prostitute in this brothel. Matangi explained to Tilopa that at this point he should begin engaging in vanquishing behavior. This outer activity, supported by the power of samadhi, is not just meditation practice, but rather a practice in which one puts oneself in lowly jobs to destroy any vestiges of arrogance. Matangi also explained that if he practiced in this way, Tilopa would attain perfect *siddhis*[11] and benefit many beings.

So Tilopa went to Bengal in eastern India and did exactly as his guru Matangi told him. During the day, he pounded sesame seeds to extract the oil and at night he was a servant to the prostitute Dharima. All the time he was engaged in this behavior outwardly his mind was completely absorbed in the samadhi of perfect suchness.

By doing this practice for twelve years Tilopa accomplished enlightenment. He was seen by people around him in different marvelous ways. Some saw him flying through the sky like a blazing ball of fire surrounded by fourteen butter lamps. Some saw him in the midst of brilliance, sitting as a yogi surrounded by women and dakinis who were circumambulating and making prostrations to him. Others saw him sitting as a bhikshu absorbed in samadhi in the midst of brilliance. When people began to see these things they started telling Dharima that something had happened to Tilopa. Dharima was really shocked at hearing this and when she went out to see for herself she saw Tilopa in the sky before her, radiant and brilliant. In his right hand he was holding the mortar and pestle for grinding sesame seeds. Dharima was upset and confessed to Tilopa that she had no idea he was such a holy person and felt very sorry that she had ordered him around as a prostitute's servant for all these years. She then offered him her deep confession.

Tilopa said, "You are not at fault. You didn't know I was a mahasiddha. Actually, I have attained all the siddhis because of you. I needed to work as your servant to become enlightened. There has been no harm done." Dharima developed great faith in Tilopa who approached her and touched her on the head with a flower. He blessed her saying, "May all the experience and wisdom I possess arise in you at this very instant." Because of her strong connection with him, she immediately had a profound experience of realization and became a *yogini*. Everyone around them was completely amazed and rejoiced. Word quickly spread to the king who came in regal splendor riding on an elephant to see what was going on. As he approached he noticed that Tilopa and Dharima were floating in the sky at the height of seven plantain trees.

Tilopa's Song of Realization

Tilopa then sang a song of realization[12] to the king and everyone assembled there, giving all the pith instructions he had received of the mother tantra, the father tantra, and the Mahamudra. Spiritual songs, *dohas*, are sung using metaphors. Tilopa began the song with an explanation that everyone knows that there is sesame oil within the sesame seed, but they don't know how to extract it. If they do not know it is to be extracted by being beaten, pressed, or cooked, they cannot obtain the pure sesame oil.

This is very similar to spiritual realization with the oil being the inborn, innate wisdom of mind. This explanation of the nature of mind is somewhat beyond the view explained in the Madhyamaka *Rangtong*[13] and the *Chittamatra* schools (see chart page 176). The Rangtong view basically points out that the nature of mind is actually only emptiness. The Madhyamaka *Shentong* view is similar to that of Mahamudra, which is that there is an actual essence of mind which is innate, primordial wisdom (which is recognized and actualized in practice). In the schools of the lesser viewpoint, the realization is the same but it is achieved through gradually developing one's meditation through progressive stages and deepening one's view. In the Mahamudra view, merely by hearing the explanation and receiving the introduction to the mind's nature as being unborn, innate spontaneous wisdom, realization can occur. With this there is recognition of all one's neurotic preconceptions which then immediately collapse into awareness itself and one attains Mahamudra directly. This is the meaning of the oil in the sesame seed.

Continuing the metaphor, there is *tathagatagarbha* which is called "*Buddha-essence*" in the sutra tradition and the "essence of primordial wisdom" in the Mahamudra tradition. Buddha-essence is found in the minds of all sentient beings. Just as you cannot extract sesame oil unless you know the process, you can't actualize the unborn natural wisdom of Mahamudra without instructions from a qualified guru. This can take place in a myriad of ways. Some gurus may point out the mind's true nature merely by explaining what it is and saying, "Your mind is Mahamudra." Others may explain it through symbols or *mudras* (hand gestures). Some may explain it in a completely special way such as when Tilopa hit Naropa in the face with his sandal or when Naropa introduced the nature of the mind to Marpa by creating a mandala of a yidam in the sky. Even though there are numerous ways of introducing the nature of mind, it is impossible to actualize this wisdom without the introduction.

Tilopa continued by singing, "By means of this magical realization of mind's nature, all experiences and awareness become inseparable, so that all phenomena and mind become inseparable. This is extremely wonderful. Kyeho! How wonderful that this is true." He concluded the spiritual song by explaining that this very simple and most wonderful of all realizations is extremely difficult to understand by any other means and may require a great deal of time in lesser traditions.

This primordial unborn wisdom of the Buddha-essence can be realized analytically or directly. In the analytical way, the Kagyu school uses the Shentong of the *Madhyamaka* view to realize the Buddha-essence. However, there is an enormous difference between Shentong and the Mahamudra approach regarding emptiness. The Shentong uses logical analysis to discover the nature of mind by deducing that "the mind is like this," using descriptive awareness to explain the unexplainable concept. However, the Mahamudra view uses experience itself and depends upon direct observation of the nature of mind under the direction of the guru. At that point one merely dwells in mind's essence experiencing it fully through direct experience.

4

Tilopa Receives Secret Instructions

The biography of Tilopa has two levels: there is the unshared biography in which it is assumed that Tilopa was a direct emanation of Vajradhara and the shared biography in which it is assumed he is a normal person and relied on worldly teachers for his training. The first part of the namtar already discussed his meeting with four great lamas. The second part concerns Tilopa's direct experience of Vajradhara, that is, meeting the wisdom dakinis and receiving instructions and teachings directly from them through visions. These two sides of the biography in no way conflict with each other. Actually, the whole story of Tilopa is quite inconceivable. It would be foolish to attempt to put all of these events in some kind of order and to state, "At this specific time Tilopa received this particular instruction from such and such a lama and had the vision of this particular wisdom dakini." These things happened simultaneously and have no chronological order. It is quite possible that Tilopa was receiving direct visionary experience from the wisdom dakinis while he was searching for a teacher on the worldly level.

The section from the unshared biography begins with how Tilopa obtained the instructions from the secret treasure house of the wisdom dakinis in the western realm of Urgyen.[14]

While Tilopa was still a youth, he was sitting in a wooded area under a tree taking care of a herd of cattle and studying the alphabet by himself in accordance with the Indian tradition of those times. A wisdom dakini appeared to him in the form of a very ugly old woman who was disgusting to look at. She asked him, "Who is your father? What is your country? What book are you reading? What are these cattle?" and so on. Tilopa answered, "My country is the Land of Zahor. My father is the Brahmin Zalwa, my mother is the Brahmin Zaldinpa, and my sister is Zaldren." He also answered other questions saying that the cattle he was taking care of were the source of his wealth and that he was reading the book to learn the dharma.

This hag became extremely angry with him and said, "You know nothing. This isn't true! Your land and country is the western realm of Urgyen. Your father is Chakrasamvara. Your mother is Vajrayogini and I am your sister. My name is Determa." Then she said, "The place where you are sitting is amidst the *bodhi trees* and the herd you need to take care of are the degrees of samadhi. The dharma you are studying is the inexpressible dharma of the *whispered lineage*. The dharma you are reading is in the hands of the wisdom dakinis."

He asked the wisdom dakini, "Will I be able to obtain teachings of this whispered lineage?" She answered, "You have three prophesied qualities of having perfect *samaya* and being an emanation[15] yourself." She continued, "With these three qualities you are entitled to go to the western land of Urgyen and demand the teachings directly from the wisdom dakinis there. In order to get there you need three things: a crystal ladder, a bridge adorned with precious jewels, and a magical key made of grass."

The items mentioned in this story are, of course, symbolic. For instance in the life story of Padmasambhava it was predicted that there would arise many obstacles to his receiving the dharma. He wanted to go to the hidden realm called Beyu which required a special way to enter. There was a raging river which no one could cross with any ferry, and there was a tree at one side of the river which was the gate to this secret kingdom. The tree couldn't be cut down with any kind of axe or sword. However, at the base of the tree was a crystal knife and the tree could be cut down with this crystal knife. When the tree fell across the river, it would serve as a bridge to the hidden kingdom in which there were many kinds of precious metals in this pure land of nirmanakaya-sambhogakaya-dharmakaya. The adept capable of going through the process of cutting the tree could attain many kinds of samadhi and great teachings in this realm. Khenpo Ganchar wrote a treatise about this particular realm. He said some people think they can just go find the river nobody can cross, see the tree, and chop it down and cross the river. He explains that this is impossible for someone who has accumulated negative *karma*. He also writes that in the literal sense a river impossible to cross does not exist and a tree that can't be cut down with an iron axe and yet can be cut down with a glass knife also doesn't exist. He then shows that these parts of the story are symbolic. The incredible torrent that can't be crossed is the turbulence of samsara. The tree that can't be cut down by ordinary means is the tree of ego-clinging. The crystal knife nestled in the tree of ego-clinging is the knife of wisdom. This metaphor shows that the practice of dharma involves traversing samsara by means of walking over one's ego-clinging. At the beginning of the path, ego-fixation is an integral part of the practice. Then traversing over this tree of ego-clinging is the path itself, and entering into the wondrous hidden kingdom of the nirmanakaya-sambhogakaya-dharmakaya is the richness of the fruition one may accomplish after completing the path. As can be seen, these symbolic stories are very profound.

I believe that this story of Tilopa is also symbolic. The crystal ladder is a metaphor for the pure view of realizing emptiness which is like a crystal. The jeweled bridge is a metaphor for meditation because meditation on resting the mind is so uncommon that it is like a bridge and it is covered with jewels because it is very pure. The grass key is a metaphor that indicates action without attachment. The key is made of grass because one doesn't become attached to something made of grass. The key is actually the key of mastering the subtle channels and energy flow within the body.

Tilopa Visits Urgyen

In accordance with the prophecy of the wisdom dakini, Tilopa asked permission to go to Urgyen from his parents. He told them he had received the prophecy that he was to go to the western realm of Urgyen and receive instructions from the wisdom dakinis there. His mother and father assented. So, he went to the western realm of Urgyen and confronted many dakinis who projected all kinds of wrathful images and frightful manifestations at him. He was very proud of the fact that he was able to overcome any fear they projected at him and wasn't afraid in the slightest of their manifestations. He went past the stages of the nirmanakaya dakinis and the sambhogakaya dakinis into the very heart of the mandala – the dharmakaya court in the center of the realm of Urgyen. He entered without fear of the terrifying experiences these dakinis were able to produce and reached the center of this mandala.

As Tilopa entered the center of the mandala, he sat down comfortably without any inhibition before Bhagavati, the great mother of all the dakinis. All the other *dakas* and dakinis were very upset that he should just stride into the center of the mandala without offering any respect to the mother of all Buddhas. They voiced this opinion to the Bhagavati and she said, "He is in fact the father of all Buddhas; he is the emanation of Chakrasamvara himself. Even if you were to produce a huge rain or hail storm of *vajras*, he would not be harmed in any way. He has every right to sit with me without offering obeisance." So the dakas and dakinis settled back in their places to witness the next stage.

The mother of all Buddhas asked Tilopa, "What do you want? Why did you come to this western realm of Urgyen?" He answered, "My sister, the wisdom dakini, told me I should come here to receive the special unwritten pith instructions that come from the lineage of direct hearing. I have come here for them, so please give them to me." Then Bhagavati made three symbolic gestures. The first symbol she made was the "tsakali," a physical symbol. Then she said a seed syllable for the speech symbol and following that she made a hand gesture (Skt. *mudra*) as the mind symbol.

Tilopa knew what these symbols meant and knew he had to explain their meaning in order to go further. He also knew exactly what to ask for and how to ask for it. He said, "I recognize that this tsakali is the treasury of the body, of the physical experience. I need to receive all the instructions of the lineage from the dharmakaya manifestation of Vajradhara himself for this." Hearing the seed syllable he recognized that this represented the treasury of speech. From the great treasury of speech he requested all the teachings, all the empowerments, and all the different degrees of practice of the path of ripening. Seeing the mudra, he recognized that it was the symbol of the treasury of mind. He asked Bhagavati for all the teachings on Mahamudra, the path of liberation.[16] He requested all these teachings of the path of ripening and the path of liberation by directly understanding the meaning of the symbols.

Bhagavati replied, "It is true. In my treasure house is the body where the wish-fulfilling jewel of the lineage lies. But the door to this treasure house is closed with the lock of samaya. Those who don't have the key of samaya cannot enter. It is true that in my treasure house of speech are the teachings of the path of ripening. All the yidam deities in this treasure house are closed to those who don't have a prophecy. It is true that in my treasure house of the mind there is the dharmakaya which contains all the correct instructions of the Mahamudra, the path of instantaneous liberation. But this is closed to those who have not attained full accomplishment."

The treasure house should not be thought of as an actual place that can be entered with a key. What this passage means is that if one has perfect samaya and has received a command that predicts one's enlightenment[17] and has accomplished a deep level of realization, these treasures and the richness of the pith instructions are available like an open door in which one can take whatever instructions one wants. Without perfect samaya, one cannot receive the legacy of this lineage. Without the prophecy, one cannot receive all the teachings of the path of ripening. Without the direct experience of the nature of *dharmata*, one cannot understand the Mahamudra.

Tilopa replied to Bhagavati, "My sister the dakini gave me a key to get into these treasure houses." At this, Bhagavati, the dakas and dakinis roared with laughter. Bhagavati responded laughingly, "A blind man can't see an image. A deaf man can't hear a sound. A mute can't talk and a cripple can't stand up and run. So whatever prophecy or key you have is from some kind of demon and is a fake." Tilopa was unperturbed by all this joking and replied, "I have the first key, the key of perfect samaya because I have recognized the self-arisen clear nature of mind. I have the second key of the prophecy because I have recognized mind as Mahamudra, the dharmata itself. I have the third key of actual accomplishment because, having merged mind totally with the dharma essence, I have direct continuous experience. So, I am fully authorized to enter the treasury."

The Bhagavati was extremely impressed with Tilopa and said, "You are the father of all Buddhas; you are the actual emanation of Chakrasamvara. You have the prophecy, the perfect samaya, and are fully accomplished. Therefore, I bestow upon you these jewels from each of my three treasuries." So she revealed to him these three jewels. Tilopa understood them instantly, saying, "Through these three jewels from the three treasure houses I will accomplish enlightenment. I am fearless and fly in the sky like a bird and there is nothing that can obstruct me. I am Sherab Sangpo (Tibetan for "deep wisdom and good"). Subsequently, Tilopa has been known as Tilopa Sherab Sangpo.

The Bhagavati and all the dakas and dakinis told Tilopa, "You must reside with us here in the land of Urgyen." Tilopa answered, "No I cannot. I have my disciples – Naropa, Rerepa, and Kasuriva – and I must take these three jewels from the treasury to bestow them upon my many disciples." Having said this, he left the land of Urgyen and was constantly followed by nine formless dakinis, who made a prophecy that he would accomplish all attainments and be able to guide and help all sentient beings.

In this way, these teachings or pith instructions that Tilopa brought from the land of Urgyen became extremely wide-spread in the land of Tibet.

5

Tilopa Gains Eight Pupils

The main disciple of Tilopa was the great Naropa. However, the whole story of Tilopa accepting Naropa as his student and the story of all the difficulties while training Naropa is not given in any detail in Tilopa's spiritual biography because it is so vividly described in Naropa's spiritual biography.[18]

Naropa was a prince and an extremely learned scholar. Consequently, he was arrogant and had a great deal of pride. For Naropa to progress along the path, Tilopa had to destroy his arrogance. Naropa was already extremely wise and had mastered a great deal of knowledge, so in Naropa's training Tilopa does not give Naropa empowerments or specific teachings. Tilopa provided an environment for Naropa to destroy his pride and arrogance by giving him all kinds of hardships to undergo.

The actual transmission of teachings to Naropa took place through symbols. The actual empowerment that did take place was with Tilopa's skill at using symbols and thus subduing Naropa's pride. Finally Naropa achieved realization with the slap of a shoe across his face by Tilopa. Naropa's wisdom and realization somehow naturally manifested by means of Tilopa's way of dealing with him.

Unlike Naropa, the eight disciples mentioned in this particular spiritual biography did not have a natural inclination towards practicing dharma and had to be subdued through miracles and magical displays.

The first of these eight main disciples of Tilopa became a disciple because a certain king was always concerned about his mother's happiness. He asked his mother, "How can I make you happy?" His mother replied, "We must gather all the *panditas* and mahasiddhas and yogis together and sponsor a great feast offering (Skt. *ganachakra*) ceremony." So the king made the arrangements but in the *ganachakra* ceremony someone has to act as the master of ceremonies (Tib. *tsog pon*). They decided that the master of ceremonies should be the great yogin Marti who was a renowned and accomplished yogi. He naturally accepted the position of master of ceremonies. But Tilopa's ugly sister appeared and told the assembly, "You've got the wrong person in charge of this ganachakra ceremony." They replied, "Who then do you think should be the leader?" She answered, "My brother Tilopa," and then she vanished.

A few minutes later she returned with Tilopa and this started a contest between Tilopa and Marti to see who was, in fact, to be the best master of ceremony. In the beginning of the contest Tilopa equaled all of the miraculous displays that Marti performed. Finally at the end of this contest Tilopa made the sun and moon fall to the ground, turned his body completely inside-out, revealing whole universes in each of his pores. At that point Marti realized he was no match for this great yogi. He developed great faith in Tilopa and requested transmission. Tilopa agreed and gave him all the pith instructions and empowerments he requested. Thus the mahasiddha Marti became the first of Tilopa's eight renowned disciples.

During this time the Buddhists were having a great deal of trouble in southern India because there was an extremely clever and erudite Hindu who was defeating them in debate. According to the tradition of those times, whoever loses a debate had to reject his own teachings and convert to the religion of the winner. Therefore, the Buddhists were suffering terribly. Tilopa received news of this and headed there disguised as a monk. When he arrived where the Hindu was causing all the trouble, he was extremely rude to the Hindu, irritating him. The Hindu said, "I challenge you to debate. If I lose, then I will reject my teachings and

Tilopa Gains Eight Disciples

convert to yours. If you lose, the same applies to you." He was fairly confident that he would win. However, Tilopa won the debate. The Hindu then displayed his miraculous power by trying to make the sun set by pushing it down towards the western horizon. Tilopa quite easily changed the direction of the sun and kept it from setting. When the sun returned to its normal position, Tilopa made the sun set and no matter how much the Hindu tried to make the sun come back up again, he had no influence on it. So he lost and admitted that he had. At this point Tilopa pulled out a knife and told the Hindu, "Now I am going to give you a haircut because you have to enter the Buddhist way which requires the cutting of your hair."[19] The Hindu was really upset about this and ran away while Tilopa chased after him. The Hindu then turned around and from his mouth a blaze of fire burned Tilopa. Tilopa returned the fire with more of his own fire, which was much more powerful than the Hindu's fire. Tilopa's fire mixed with the Hindu's fire and turned toward the Hindu, who became severely burned. At this point he gave up and the Hindu Nagpogowa became the second of Tilopa's great disciples.

The third disciple was found because the kingdoms in Bengal were extremely rich at that time and were under attack from an extremely vicious and deceitful magician. This magician had been progressing through various kingdoms in the south of India creating with magic enormous armies and causing these kingdoms to surrender out of fear of war. After he robbed and pillaged the palaces of one kingdom, he continued on to the next kingdom using his magical power to defeat his enemies. In a city of one of the kingdoms of Bengal the magician arrived with his horde of magically produced armies and all the people in the city were extremely frightened and had a large meeting to discuss what they should do in the face of this attack.

Then along came Tilopa's ugly old sister and told those gathered at the meeting, "What are you doing?" They answered, "We are deciding what to do about this invasion." She suggested, "You can't win unless you use the services of my brother." They asked where he was and she answered, "He is waltzing with corpses in the charnel ground." Tilopa had attached corpses to a horse hair left in the branches of a huge tree. Of course, the citizens did not believe her and thought she was crazy. But they decided to take a look anyway and when they did, they saw Tilopa doing exactly what the hag had said. He was dancing with corpses hanging from a single horse hair. Seeing that he must have magical power to do this, they invited him to their city to defend the realm. Tilopa, by the power of his samadhi, completely dissolved the magical illusion created by the magician, grabbed hold of him, and threw him into jail. This magician then became the third of Tilopa's main disciples.

The fourth disciple was a woman who ran a brewery in central India with the help of a young servant. She had become very famous for the quality of her beer and was extremely proud and attached to her business. One day when the young male servant was away from the brewery, Tilopa entered the brewery and began pulling all the stoppers out of the kegs of beer, letting it flow onto the ground. The woman was infuriated and very abusive towards Tilopa who then disappeared. The lady then sat down weeping over her fate of having lost all of her wonderful beer. The young servant returned, and having heard what had happened, shouted, "We should kill the person who did this." At this point Tilopa transformed himself into a cat and began jumping among the beer barrels, pulling out the rest of the stoppers until the entire supply of beer was gone. The woman and the young servant began chasing the cat, trying to beat it, but it always jumped out of the way because it was a manifestation of Tilopa. Both were completely in despair when Tilopa came strolling in nonchalantly saying, "What's the matter with you? Why are you so upset?" The woman answered, "You've ruined my supply of beer. You have destroyed my whole business and I have no more livelihood." Tilopa replied, "No, wait. Look inside the barrels and you will see that they are refilled with even better beer." She didn't believe this, but went to see. She found that all the barrels were full of a wonderful new brew. Then she had instantaneous great faith in Tilopa and became his fourth disciple.

Tilopa Gains Eight Disciples

At another time Tilopa heard of a butcher who slaughtered animals for a living. He wanted to make him his disciple so he entered the butcher's premises and with a magical trick made the lower side of beef that was cooking in the pot look like the butcher's son and then left. The butcher came home and wanted to look at the meat that was boiling all day, lifted up the lid and there was his only son, well cooked in the pot. He was completely heart-broken and was so depressed that he couldn't do anything more for seven days. Tilopa had caused the actual son to disappear from the scene and Tilopa arrived at the end of seven days. When he returned he saw the butcher crying and asked, "What's the matter with you?" The butcher said, "You did it. You killed my son and put him in the cooking pot and now he is dead." Tilopa replied, "Well, look at how much suffering you had to undergo by being a father and seeing your child killed. Don't you think that the father and mothers of animals suffer seeing their children being taken away from them and slaughtered?" The butcher was then moved from his depression and said, "This is really true. I've caused so much suffering to those mothers of the animals I've butchered." Tilopa said, "If I could bring back your son, would you completely give up your work as a butcher?" The butcher replied, "Without a doubt I would if you can bring back my son." So Tilopa brought the son out of hiding and said, "This is your son who is alive again." At this point the butcher developed great faith in Tilopa, received all the teachings and instructions from him, and became his fifth major disciple, the mahasiddha Gawa.

The next disciple lived in Srinagara in India. He was a very great singer who was very famous and proud of his accomplishments. He traveled from town to town receiving payment for his great performances and enjoyed the great deal of applause and was very arrogant about his talent. So one day he was in Srinagara singing his heart out in the middle of the village when Tilopa came from the other side of the square singing even more beautiful and sweet melodies and outdoing this most famous of singers. A battle arose between them with Tilopa having manifested himself as a singer. No matter how sweetly the song sounded, the singer couldn't sing better than Tilopa. Then he said, "Until now I thought I was the greatest singer in the whole world. Now I've met you I see that you must be a god, a *naga* or some other kind of spirit. How is it that you can possibly have such a wonderful singing voice?" Tilopa then showed his real form and the singer was so astounded with this miraculous display that he requested to become his disciple. Tilopa assented and bestowed upon him the teachings and instructions. The singer became the sixth famous disciple called Yontan.

The seventh disciple of Tilopa was found when Tilopa heard about an on-going debate between a great Hindu scholar and a Buddhist scholar who were always debating the law of cause and effect (karma). The debate went on for a long time with each side using great logic. At every turn of the argument, the Hindu scholar refuted the law of karma, which is the cornerstone of the Buddhist viewpoint. Tilopa heard about this and entered the debate. He said, "Listen, you two don't have to continue the debate. Just take hold of my garment and I'll show you something." As soon as they took hold of his garment with one on the left and one on the right, Tilopa took them to the hell realms with all its intense suffering. In particular there were great cauldrons full of boiling iron with the hell beings being tortured and screaming in the pot of molten metal. They were being stirred around by a guardian of the hell realm. Then Tilopa asked, "What is it they have done to experience such great suffering?" The guardian of the hell realm answered, "These are people who did not believe in the law of karma. They have therefore developed many negative tendencies and did many evil deeds. The result of these actions is birth in the midst of this boiling metal." The Hindu at this point was terrified and said, "Oh, I was wrong. It's true about the law of karma." He looked around and there was another cauldron completely empty of beings, but full of boiling metal. He then asked the guardian, "What is this one for? Why is it empty?" The guardian said, "We are preparing this for those people who have refuted the law of karma." The Hindu was then extremely terrified and gave up all doubts about the law of karma and thought that he had actually died and said, "Is this it? Is this the moment I'm to be born in the hell realms?"

Tilopa Gains Eight Disciples

Tilopa then went to one of the heavenly realms[20] with the two scholars still holding onto his garment and made them witness an orgy of sensual delights of the god realm. The Hindu looked at this and asked why these beings were experiencing such pleasure and happiness. The reply came, "It's because these people have practiced great virtue and developed their noble qualities. The result of this is the blissful experience of the god realm." Just over to one side there was a celestial palace empty with a harem of gorgeous women in it. The Hindu asked, "Why is no one there to enjoy this?" They said that they were preparing for the future bliss of those who had a strong belief in the law of karma and were developing the noble qualities of practicing virtuous behavior." The Hindu was then completely convinced of the law of karma and become Tilopa's seventh major disciple, called Nagatanga.

Tilopa realized that he had to go to one more place to subjugate a great sorcerer who was extremely vicious and sadistic and loved to use his black magic upon the terrified population. He liked to cast spells on people, curse and kill them in their tracks, and generally loved causing great harm so that everyone was afraid of him. Tilopa traveled to where he was and said something extremely rude to the sorcerer who was delighted at another opportunity to perform his evil magic. He said to Tilopa, "I'm going to cast a spell on you." Tilopa replied, "Go right ahead. What kind of power do you have that you can cast a spell on me?" So the sorcerer cast a spell as hard as he could while Tilopa just sat there and watched the spell taking place. As it took place, all of the sorcerer's relatives fell sick and died because Tilopa had turned the power of the magic spell upon them. Tilopa then said to the sorcerer, "Well, you did your magic and I don't even have a toothache. But look at your relatives, they're all dead." Then the sorcerer was so overwrought and began crying and weeping. "Look how much you're suffering because your magic has caused the death of all your relatives." Tilopa then added, "If I could revive all your relatives, would you have faith in me and abandon your ways?" The sorcerer insisted that he would never again do any black magic. Tilopa then revived all his relatives and the sorcerer became the eighth important disciple of Tilopa and was called Siddha Nidazingpa, which in Tibetan means "the eclipse of the sun and moon."

PART II

The Ganges Mahamudra: Oral Instructions on Mahamudra

THRANGU TASHI CHÖLING,
NEPAL, 1994

The Root Text

Ganges Mahamudra

Homage to the Vajradakini

Although Mahamudra cannot be taught, intelligent and patient Naropa, tolerant of suffering, who is engaged in austerity and is devoted to the guru, fortunate one, do this with your mind.

For example, in space what is resting on what? In one's mind, Mahamudra, there is nothing to be shown. Rest relaxed in the natural state without attempting to alter anything. If this fetter or bondage of thought is loosened, there is no doubt that you will be liberated.

For example, it is like looking in the middle of the sky and not seeing anything. In the same way, when your mind looks at your mind, thoughts stop and you attain unsurpassable awakening.

For example, just as the vapor that, arising from the earth, becomes clouds and dissolves into the expanse of space, not going anywhere else and yet not continuing to abide anywhere, in the same way the agitation of the thoughts that arise from the mind and within the mind is calmed the instant you see the mind's nature.

For example, just as the nature of space transcends color and shape, and just as space is therefore unaffected or unchanged and unobscured by the various colors and shapes that occur within it, in the same way the essence of your mind transcends color and shape, and therefore, is never obscured or affected by the various colors and shapes of virtue and wrongdoing.

For example, it is like the luminous heart of the sun, which could never be obscured even by the darkness of a thousand eons. In that way, that luminous clarity that is the essence of the mind is never obscured by the samsara of innumerable kalpas.

For example, just as we apply the term empty to space, in fact, there is nothing within space that we are accurately describing by that term. In the same way, although we call the mind clear light or luminosity, simply calling it so does not make it true that there is actually any thing within the mind that is a true basis for that designation.

In that way, the nature of the mind has from the beginning been like space, and there are no dharmas that are not included within that.

Abandoning all physical actions, the practitioner should rest at ease. Without any verbal utterance, your speech becomes like an echo, sound inseparable from emptiness. Think of nothing whatsoever with the mind and look at the dharmas of the leap.

The body is without meaning, empty like a bamboo stalk. The mind is like the midst of space. It is inconceivable. Rest relaxed within that, without letting it go or placing it. Rest relaxed in that state without sending it out or placing it in, letting it go or attempting to place it.

If mind has no direction, it is Mahamudra. With this you will attain unsurpassable awakening.

Those who follow tantra and the vehicle of the paramitas, the Vinaya, the Sutras, and the various teachings of the Buddha with an attachment for their individual textual traditions and their individual philosophy will not come to see luminous Mahamudra. Because the seeing of that luminosity or clear light is obscured by their intention and attitude.

The conceptualized maintenance of vows actually causes you to impair the meaning of samaya. Without mental directedness or mental activity, be free of all intentionality. Thoughts are self-arisen and self-pacified like designs on the surface of water. If you do not pass beyond the meaning which is not abiding and not conceptualizing or focusing, then through not passing beyond that, you do not pass beyond or transgress samaya. This is the torch which dispels all obscurity or darkness.

If free of all intention you do not abide in extremes, you will see without exception the meaning of all the Buddha's teachings or of all the sections of the Buddha's teachings.

If you rest in this, you will be liberated from the prison of samsara. If you rest evenly within this, all of your wrongdoing and obscurations will be burned. This is called for those reasons the torch of the doctrine.

Foolish people who have no interest in this will only be continually carried off by the river of samsara. Those foolish people experiencing intolerable sufferings in lower states of existence are worthy of compassion.

Wishing to attain liberation from intolerable suffering, rely upon a wise guru. When the guru's blessings enter your heart, your mind will be liberated. These things of samsara are meaningless or pointless, the causes of suffering. And since all of these things that have been done or made are pointless, look at that which is meaningful.

If you are beyond all grasping at an object and grasping at a subject, that is the monarch of all views. If there is no distraction, it is the monarch among all meditations. If there is no effort, that is the monarch among all conducts. When there is no hope and no fear, that is the final result, and the fruition has been attained or revealed.

It is beyond being an object of conceptual focus, and the mind's nature is lucidity. There is no path to be traversed and yet, in that way you enter the path to Buddhahood. There is no object of meditation, but if you become accustomed to this, you will attain unsurpassable awakening.

Thoroughly examine mundane things or the things of the world. If you do, you will see that none of them persist, none of them are capable of permanence, and in that sense, they are like dreams and magical illusions. Dreams and magical illusions are meaningless. Therefore, generate renunciation and abandon mundane concerns.

Cut through the bonds of attachment and aversion toward those around you and your surroundings. Meditate in isolated retreats, forests, and so forth, living alone. Remain in that state without meditation. When you attain that which is without attainment, you have attained Mahamudra.

For example, if the single root of a tree with a trunk and many branches, leaves, flowers and fruit is cut, the ten thousand or one hundred thousand branches will automatically die. In the same way, if the root of mind is cut through, the branches and leaves of samsara will dry up.

For example, just as the darkness that has accumulated over a thousand eons is dispelled by the illumination of one lamp or one torch, in the same way, one instant of the wisdom of the clear light of one's mind dispels all of the ignorance, wrongdoing and obscurations accumulated throughout numerous eons.

Kye ho

The intellect cannot see that which is beyond conceptual mind. You will never realize that which is uncreated through created dharmas. If you wish to attain or realize that which is beyond the intellect and is uncreated, then scrutinize your mind and strip awareness naked.

Allow the cloudy water of thought to clarify itself or to clear itself. Do not attempt to stop or create appearances. Leave them as they are. If you are without acceptance and rejection of external appearances, all that appears and exists will be liberated as mudra.

The all-basis is unborn, and without that unborn all-basis, abandon or relinquish habits, wrongdoing, and obscurations. Therefore, do not fixate or reckon. Rest in the essence of the unborn or in the unborn nature. In that state, appearances are fully apparent; but within that experience of vivid appearances allow concepts to be exhausted or to dissolve.

Complete liberation from all conceptual extremes is the supreme monarch of views. Boundless vastness is the supreme monarch of meditations. Being directionless and utterly impartial is the supreme monarch of conduct. Self-liberation beyond expectation or hope is the supreme result or fruition.

For a beginner it is like a fast current running through a narrow bed or a narrow defile. In the middle or after that, it becomes like the gentle current of the River Ganges. In the end, it is like the flowing of all rivers into the mother ocean, or it is like the meeting of the mother and child of all the rivers.

Those of little intelligence, if they find they cannot remain in that state, may apply or hold the technique of the breathing and emphasize the essence of awareness. Through many techniques or branches such as gaze and holding the mind, tighten awareness until it stays put, exerting tension or effort until awareness comes to rest in that state or in its nature.

If you rely upon karmamudra, the wisdom of bliss and emptiness will arise. Enter into the union having consecrated the upaya or method and the prajna or knowledge. Slowly let it fall or send it down, coil it, turn it back, and lead it to its proper place. Finally spread it or cause it to pervade your whole body. If there is no attachment or craving, the wisdom of bliss and emptiness will appear.

You will possess longevity without white hair and you will be as healthy as the waxing moon. Your complexion will be lustrous and you will be as powerful as a lion. You will quickly attain the common siddhis or attainments, and you will come to alight in or attain the supreme siddhi as well.

The Root Text

These instructions of the essential point of Mahamudra, may they abide in the hearts of worthy or fortunate beings.

Colophon

This was bestowed on the banks of the River Ganges by the great and Glorious Siddha Tilopa, who had realized Mahamudra, upon the Kashmiri pandit who was both learned and realized, Naropa, after Naropa had engaged in twelve hardships or austerities. This was translated and written down at Pullahari in the north by the great Naropa and the great Tibetan translator, the king among translators, Marpa Chokyi Lodro.

This is a translation of the root text by
Lama Yeshe Gyamtso during the course of teaching by Thrangu Rinpoche

Master Tilopa and Master Naropa

6

Introduction to The Ganges Mahamudra

The text that I am going to explain is called "Ganges Mahamudra." It was taught by Tilopa to Naropa; then it was taught by Naropa to Lord Marpa, who translated it into Tibetan, thus giving us the text that we use. This short text of instruction is considered the root text or source text of all *Kagyu* doctrine in general, and especially of our tradition of Mahamudra. So I feel very fortunate to have the opportunity to explain it to you, and I thank you all for giving me this opportunity.

Mahamudra is an approach to practice that can be used by any person, by anyone at all. It is an approach that engulfs any practitioner with tremendous splendor that is very effective and very easy to implement. This is especially true in the present time and is also especially true for the people of the West, for whom there appear to be very few obstacles in the practice of Mahamudra. It was for this reason that in order to propagate the teachings of the Buddha in general and of the Kagyu tradition in particular, His Holiness the Sixteenth Karmapa, Tralung Rigpe Dorje, with great inconvenience to himself went to the West on several occasions. When he was teaching in the West and spreading the Buddha-dharma there, he was asked by students, "Since the Kagyu teachings are now spreading throughout the world, what texts should be translated?" His Holiness answered that the first major text of great importance should be the text known as *Moonbeams of Mahamudra* by Dagpo Tashi Namgyal.[21] It should be translated as soon as possible because it is a very important source text for the study and practice of Mahamudra. So in accordance with His Holiness' vision, this was done and is now a book that is readily available.

From time to time I have suggested and encouraged students to read *Moonbeams of Mahamudra* and said, "It is a very good book. You should read it." Often people respond, "Well, it is too long and it doesn't seem to be so important. It is too dry," or something like that. So to encourage people to actually make use of this text, I have taught it extensively. However, it is the case that it is a text of vast scope and some length, so in order to suit the needs of those who need a more abbreviated explanation of Mahamudra I teach this present text, *The Ganges Mahamudra*, which is concise and full of splendor.

What makes Mahamudra so special? There are these extremely profound practices such as the "Six limbs of the completion stage of the Kalachakra tantra" and of course the renowned instructions of *Dzogchen* ("the great perfection") – and these are really special, but for ordinary practitioners there seems to be some problem of implementing them. For example, sometimes people try to practice Dzogchen in the format of a dark retreat. It is possible by spending a month or two in total darkness to generate uncommon experiences and realization – it is also quite possible that an ordinary person might go completely nuts. Or if people practice the more conventional *tögal* (Tibetan for "leap-over") using the rays of sunlight as an external condition, it is possible that through the profundity of such a technique that extraordinary and ensuing wisdom might be generated – but sometimes people who try this practice don't do it right and then run in saying that they are going blind. Mahamudra, in contrast to such techniques, has no such dangers. It is a practice that does not bring madness, that can be undertaken in a state of relaxation, and in a state of ease. Mahamudra then is an approach to dharma that embodies great blessing, great splendor.

The term Mahamudra in Sanskrit was translated into Tibetan as *phyag-gya-chen-po*. *Maha* means "great" and *mudra* means "a seal," for example, the seal of a king affixed to a proclamation by that king. At the same time, the second syllable of *phyag-gya*, which is the translation of mudra, can also mean "vast." One of the implications of this term in

Introduction to Ganges Mahamudra

the Tibetan translation is that the nature and manifestation of all things, the emptiness of all things, are vast and unfathomable. If they are recognized, if the same nature is recognized internally, within or as the mind of the practitioner, then this recognition in its encompassing vastness seals or pervades all that person's experience in that through that recognition they recognize the nature of all things. So, that is why mudra is called "a seal," with the connotation of vastness. The reason why it is called "great seal" or Mahamudra is that this is obviously something far greater than a conventional seal, such as the monarch's seal on a document. Mahamudra is the greatest seal of all.

The Sanskrit term mudra in Mahamudra itself basically just means "a seal." And the Tibetan term *phyag-gya* means a little more than that in the sense that the siddhas who translated this from Sanskrit into Tibetan added the third syllable, the word *phyag*. Now if we look at this word *phyag* on a purely etymological or common level, it is the honorific word for "hand." However, the uncommon meaning of this in this context, which is the actual reason why the honorific is used in this term, is somewhat profound. Because *phyag* is the honorific for "hand," it is applied obviously to the hands of the Buddha, the hands of *bodhisattvas*, the hands of one's guru and so forth. However, this term is also used in an ordinary sense to refer to tools of cleaning, such as a broom, which is called a *phyag-ma*, and also a cleaner, someone who uses the broom, who might simply be called *phyag*. So the term has a connotation both of honorific and also of cleaning, of that which cleans. Putting these two connotations of this word together, you get the fact that the work or that which is done with the hands or the imprint of Buddhas, bodhisattvas and gurus is to clean, cleanse or purify the minds of the students. For example, this term could also be used of a king – the king's ministers promote a goodness or healthiness in the lives of the people they govern, which is an act of cleansing. The meaning of it then is that the practice of Mahamudra has a cleansing effect, in the sense that it purifies or cuts through one's *disturbing emotions*,[22] and that is why it is called *phyag-gya-chen-po*. So, that's the reason why Mahamudra was translated in this way.

However, when this is explained there are further implications as well. In commentaries you will find that the first syllable of the Tibetan word *phyag* means "emptiness" – it refers to emptiness, that which is realized. The second syllable *gya* (which itself could simply mean "a sea" or "vastness") refers to the wisdom of that which realizes emptiness. What has been pointed out is that these two are not separate from each other, they are not dual. Mahamudra is the inseparability of emptiness and wisdom or space and wisdom, which is indicated by the Tibetan word *chen-po,* Sanskrit *maha*, which means "great." The point is that that which is the supreme pacification of all suffering and all causes of suffering, the disturbing emotions (*kleshas*) and so forth, is this wisdom of emptiness – the emptiness itself and that which realizes it, this stable clarity of Mahamudra. And the word *chen-po, maha,* "great," which implies the non-duality of emptiness and the wisdom which recognizes emptiness, also indicates the all-pervasive quality of this experience or realization.

The Name of the Text

The text that we are studying is the instructions given by Lord Tilopa to Lord Naropa after Naropa had undergone the twelve great austerities which he underwent at Tilopa's hand. Since this was taught by Tilopa to Naropa on the banks of the River Ganges, it is called "The Ganges Mahamudra." Some texts are named after the student who requests the instruction, some texts are named after the topic, some texts are named after the place where the instruction was given. This text is named after the place, the River Ganges.

This text begins with the name of the text in Sanskrit, followed by the name of the text in Tibetan. This is always the case with texts, especially those that have been translated into Tibetan from Sanskrit. There are many reasons for this, but it would take a long time to discuss them. So I am just going to leave it with the statement that the text begins with its name in Sanskrit, translated into English.

Introduction to Ganges Mahamudra

Mahamudra Upadesha — *The Ganges Mahamudra.*

The Homage

The text proper begins with a homage. Now there are different editions of this text in Tibetan, and the first difference between the two most common editions is in this first line. In some editions it says, "Homage to glorious co-emergence," and in some it says, "Homage to the Vajradakini." The text we are using primarily is the one which begins with,

Homage to the Vajradakini

The meaning of the homage here is to Mahamudra, Prajnaparamita, in the form of the dakini or the mother, because she is the mother of all Buddhas, the realization that produces all Buddhas.

A Brief Explanation of the Text

The principal format for the study of this text is a brief topical analysis, which was composed by the Third Gyalwa Karmapa, Rangjung Dorje. In his analysis of the text, the first section or topic is the promise to teach or the undertaking of the act of teaching by the teacher, in this case Tilopa. The text begins with the statement that:

Although Mahamudra cannot be taught, intelligent and patient Naropa, tolerant of suffering, who is engaged in austerity and is devoted to the guru, fortunate one, do this with your mind.

Here "engaged in austerities" refers to the twelve minor and twelve greater austerities undergone by Naropa in his search for and initial contact with Tilopa. These twenty-four austerities are described in his biography.

It is important to understand the reason why Naropa underwent these austerities. He did not undergo them for any mundane reason, such as wanting food or clothing. He underwent them to find and please the guru. It is necessary for a student to prove to a teacher that he or she has enough confidence and trust in that teacher and in the teacher's instructions to be able to undergo such austerities, because only someone who has that much longing and trust can actually practice this kind of teaching. If he or she were to practice it, there will be a fruition; and if a student does not practice it, there will obviously be no point in the whole process. Therefore, the ability to practice depends upon the ability to undergo these austerities. And if there is no ability, no willingness to undergo such austerities, then that is an indication that there is no trust on the student's part in either the guru or the instructions of the guru.

Generally, in Buddha-dharma there is no notion that physical suffering is a prerequisite for practice and for awakening. Yet we see that in the lives of Naropa and Milarepa they both underwent inconceivable physical suffering in the process of their training. Nevertheless, they underwent this not for the sake of the suffering itself, but to show their complete trust and complete confidence in their guru. Because Naropa was absolutely certain that if he succeeded in receiving instructions from Tilopa he would attain full enlightenment or awakening, he had the courage to undergo all these austerities. So in response to that demonstration on Naropa's part Tilopa said, "Intelligent and patient Naropa, tolerant of suffering, fortunate (or worthy) one, do this with your mind." When Tilopa says, "Do this with your heart or mind,"[23] what he is saying is, "Now that you have proven yourself, if you do this, you will realize the fruition."

7

The View of Mahamudra

A Detailed Explanation of the Text

Now, going on with the text and returning to Rangjung Dorje's topical analysis, at this point I have to tell you that there are two orders in which this text can be found. Depending upon which Tibetan text you are using, you will notice that the verses are in a different order. We are going to use the order of the text which begins with "Homage to Vajradakini" and not with "Homage to glorious Co-emergence." In any case, according to Rangjung Dorje's topical analysis, there are seven topics presented in the text. In the more common order, they are the following: (1) the view of Mahamudra; (2) the conduct of Mahamudra; (3) the meditation of Mahamudra: (4) the samaya of Mahamudra; (5) the benefits of practicing Mahamudra; (6) the defects of not practicing Mahamudra, and (7) the manner of practice itself. Of these seven, we will now begin to examine the first, the view, which initially presents six similes or metaphors.

Perhaps it would be more correct to say that there are six points rather than six examples because, as you will see, space is used as a simile not only in the first of these six points presenting the view but also in the second and fourth points. This shows one of the main differences between poetic composition in general and the spontaneous composition of this type of spiritual song and instruction. When one normally composes poetry, one writes the poem or a section of it, looks at it and improves it a little bit, later on looks at it again and improves it a little bit more, editing it again and again and again. Nowadays we would do this with a computer, whereas a spiritual song is spontaneously produced, being sung by the teacher who is trying to communicate. So there is less attention paid to the restrictions of poetic traditions, the reason why the same example of space can be used again and again.

The View of Mahamudra in Six Points

1. Space as an Example of the Absence of Solidity

For example, in space what is resting on what? In one's mind, Mahamudra, there is nothing to be shown. Rest relaxed in the natural state without attempting to alter anything.

The term "without attempting to alter anything (i.e. 'without fabrication')" used here means that the practice is not an attempt to improve or alter anything; there is nothing that needs to be fixed or altered. The word "natural" here means that there is nothing that needs to be added to make this state complete and that there is nothing that needs to be removed to make this state wholesome.

The fourth line continues,

If this fetter or bondage of thought is loosened, there is no doubt that you will be liberated.

What this means is that normally we take what we experience (such as a strong arising of disturbing emotions, mental afflictions, and so forth) to be solid, to be real. This unnecessary misapprehension of the aspects of experience as truly existing is what binds us. If we can let go of and relinquish that, then that itself will bring liberation.

2. Space as an Example of when Mahamudra is Practiced

The second point concerning the view also uses space as the image.

For example, it is like looking in the middle of the sky and not seeing anything. In the same way, when your mind looks at your mind, thoughts stop and you attain unsurpassable awakening.

In the first point, space was used as an image to indicate the emptiness of Mahamudra, the absence of solidity. Here space is being used in a slightly different way, as an experiential image to communicate the idea of what happens when Mahamudra is practiced. What happens is that when the mind looks at itself, thoughts cease and there is awakening.

When we look into the middle of the empty sky, we don't see much of anything at all; nothing arises in our visual perception, there is no form that is really seen. Whereas when we look at the ground, of course we see all sorts of things. This example is used to indicate what it is like when in the practice of Mahamudra we look at what is looked at in that practice, which is our own mind. From a logical point of view, this is impossible – it makes no sense. It is like assuming that a sword can cut itself or we can stand on our own shoulders. Nevertheless in actual experience, it is not only possible, it is not that difficult. The reason is that our mind is very, very close to us; it is not something that is separated from us at all – there is nothing between us and our mind. In that sense, we could say that it is not an extremely hard thing to find because it is right there all the time – it is the same cognition, the same awareness, that we always have.

However, if this mind were a solid object and had some kind of substantiality, then when looking at it we would see something. Yet, when you look directly at our mind, we don't see anything. The Third Karmapa, Rangjung Dorje, said in *The Aspirational Prayer of Mahamudra*: "It is not existent and is not seen even by the Victorious Ones." This means that we can say from a certain point of view that there is nothing there, there is nothing to see. The reason we don't see anything when we look directly at the mind is not because it is obscured in some way; it is not that we don't know how to look or we have to overcome the obstructions to see it directly. That's why Rangjung Dorje said, "Even the Buddhas do not see it." There is a song by Gampopa in which he said, "Having certainty that this is the view, look at our own mind."

We usually divide dharma into view, meditation, and conduct. There are two approaches to the view, one is the sutra approach using reasoning. In this approach, we can generate confidence in the view through analysis and inferential reasoning. We can become confident that we have sufficiently analyzed a particular topic and that we have determined its nature. The second approach, the Vajrayana approach to the view, makes no use of inferential analysis, but is direct experience. It is this approach to the view that is referred to in these two quotations and this section of the text. In other words, from the point of direct experience, seeing the mind directly and yet not seeing anything is possible.

There is a distinction to be made between the practice of *tranquillity meditation* and the practice of Mahamudra, particularly in regard to how thoughts are viewed and treated. In the practice of tranquillity meditation, thoughts are basically viewed as enemies and we want to eliminate them somehow. Sometimes by being trained in the practice and using the effective antidotes employed in tranquillity meditation, we succeed in thoughts dissolving. Then sometimes we don't succeed and we fight with them. In the practice of Mahamudra, we do not do this because whatever aspect of mind we are talking about (the *eight consciousnesses*; the alaya consciousness, the afflicted consciousness, the mental consciousness or the five sensory consciousnesses) there is a clarity or lucidity that arises in these various ways as mental events, as types of consciousness. When we look directly at the mind that is the basis of this clarity, it seems to be nothing; we don't see any solid thing, yet there is a clarity. This experience of there being nothing when we look at the mind is what is described in the second turning of the *wheel of dharma* and the Madhyamaka (Middle-way) tradition as the *dharmadhatu* and emptiness. In this case, even though thoughts may be present as an expression of that clarity, nevertheless when we see that there is nothing there, thoughts automatically cease on their own without having to be intentionally altered, without viewing them as enemies or without attempting to diminish them.

How does this actually happen, that looking at the mind somehow causes thoughts to dissolve? There was a very important Terton called Yongge-Migji-Dorje; who discovered a *sadhana* called "Sampopang" or "Proper Container." In that liturgy, it talks about the essence or nature of anger. The point that is made is that anger only has any meaningful sense if it is outwardly directed. We can't have anger that is not outwardly directed, which means that if we turn anger in on itself, if we who are angry look directly at our anger then there doesn't seem to be anything. We can't find where the anger is. We can't find what shape it has, we can't find what color it has, nor any substantial qualities to it. If anger, for example, has none of these substantial qualities, then what does it have? What could it possibly be? What we think of as being "anger" is merely the appearance of anger and not really anything at all. It is like looking at the wind while asking for the sky – we can't see anything. So if we look at our own anger, then we won't see it, and that produces pacification of this anger. This is also discussed in the Mahayana as well as emptiness, and in the Hinayana as the selflessness of persons. But whether or not it was taught by the Buddha, it is certainly an object of direct experience; when you look at your own mind, you can directly experience mind's essential emptiness.

This is true not only of anger but also of other mental afflictions such as desire, attachment, jealousy, pride and so forth. And it is not only true of negative thoughts but also of positive thoughts. Whatever form a thought takes, if we look directly at it, we will see that it is in its nature non-existent, and that recognition pacifies the thought or causes it to cease. Now how does this produce awakening? Normally, we do not ever look at our mind in this way. From the time we wake in the morning until the time we go to sleep our mind is just streams of one thought after another, one thought producing a second which produces a third and so forth, and that is our whole life. Not only that, but while some of these uncontrolled thoughts are virtuous, most of them are negative. Under the influence of negative thoughts we engage in harmful actions which cause us to wander around and around through the *three realms* of samsara and to be completely miserable. We can see that in fact thoughts that are expressions of delight and uplifted happenings are comparatively rare for us. We spend most of our time thinking about how miserable we are. Well, if we rest in Mahamudra, all of that stops. It is through that process of stopping that we gradually come to accomplish awakening.

Those three lines, ["For example, it is like looking in the middle of the sky and not seeing anything. In the same way, when your mind looks at your mind, thoughts stop and you attain unsurpassable awakening."] are again the image of space, in this case to point out the process of the pacification of thoughts.

3. Mist Illustrating the Way Thoughts Dissolve

The third point uses a slightly different image, which is mist or clouds. They are used as an image illustrating the way thoughts dissipate or dissolve of themselves:

For example, just as the vapor that, arising from the earth, becomes clouds and dissolves into the expanse of space, not going anywhere else and yet not continuing to abide anywhere, in the same way the agitation of the thoughts that arise from the mind and within the mind is calmed the instant you see the mind's nature.

In this case, what is called the main mind is that cognitive clarity or the cognitive potential, which is basically what mind is and how it manifests. When applied to the six consciousness, it means the mental consciousness. In this usage it is distinguished from that which arises from or within the mind, which are all different thoughts, conceptualizations, mental formations and experiences that we undergo, such as for example the fifty-one types of mental formations, such as the five that must be present for a volitional action, the various virtuous and unvirtuous ones and so forth.

The View of Mahamudra

What we are trying to do in the practice of tranquillity meditation is to suppress or weaken thoughts. By weakening them, which lessens the power and clarity disturbing them, we come to relax in the state of tranquillity. In the practice of Mahamudra, what happens (although not done in the same way) is that rather than thoughts being suppressed or weakened they are purified. This is done through the direct experience that your mind is something that, while it definitely can be said to have an innate cognitive clarity, has no solidity, no substantial existence. Whether you call this nature, "emptiness," "clarity," "the unity of emptiness and clarity" or "the unity of space and wisdom" the experience is not seen as something existent that does not exist nor as something non-existent that does exist. This genuine and direct experience or recognition causes the mist or waves of thought to naturally dissolve.

There is a song of Milarepa that is found in *The Rain of Wisdom,* a song of instructions given to Nima Paldenpo. This song consists of five images of which one is appropriate here. Milarepa said, "Look at the depths of the ocean and meditate without waves. Look at the mind, and meditate without thought." In response Nima Paldenpo asked Milarepa, "Well, I can look at the ocean, but what do I do with all those waves? I can look at my mind, but what do I do with all those thoughts?" This means that she can look at the mind, nevertheless she is disturbed by the thoughts arising within it. Milarepa's response was, "Well, if you can meditate on the ocean, then you can experience that the waves which arise on the ocean's surface are merely the expression of the ocean itself. If you can meditate on the mind, then the thoughts which arise are nothing other than the mind's expressions."

What this means is that if you see your own mind, then what you see is that the mind's essence or nature is emptiness. When you see that, you also see that the nature of whatever thought arises in the mind is also emptiness. When this is experienced directly, then these thoughts dissolve in their own place, which means right there or right here. Thoughts are not driven out or go somewhere else; they do not go away, they simply dissolve naturally because they are seen. So, that was the third image.

It is very important to practice these instructions both in formal meditation and also in the midst of your activities by using the practice of mindfulness. It is important to remember that each of us at the present has the extraordinary opportunity of being a human being with eighteen special characteristics.[24] Modern life is very busy and it seems we either lead a full, active and productive life, and therefore have no time to meditate, or we spend our time in the practice of meditation and are dissatisfied with the quality of our lives. So people are always saying, "Oh, I don't have time to practice," or "My life is no good." In fact, from a Mahamudra point of view, there is no such contradiction. Mahamudra should be practiced formally in sitting meditation as much as possible, but when you cannot do that, you always have the opportunity to apply these instructions in the midst of whatever activities you are performing.

There are illustrations of this in the history of our lineage, such as Tilopa who practiced continually while pounding sesame seeds for a living and through that practice attained full awakening. This is an important example for us. So practice well in that way, according to that example, and don't let yourself be overpowered by disturbing emotions.

4. Space as an Example of Changelessness

The next stanza again uses space as the image:

For example, just as the nature of space transcends color and shape, and just as space is therefore unaffected or unchanged and unobscured by the various colors and shapes that occur within it, in the same way the essence of your mind transcends color and shape, and therefore, is never obscured or affected by the various colors and shapes of virtue and wrongdoing.

Here we have to be clear about which of the various meanings of space or sky we are referring to. In the *Abhidharmakosha* the two main uses of the term "space" are explained. One is referring to "space" as something that is not anything, that is not a composite of anything and therefore has no visible characteristics and that is the space as empty space. The other use of the term "space" is to mean the sky, which is perceived as being blue. In these images we are not talking about the blue sky, so when we say that space in its nature has no color, it should not be seen as contradictory to the fact that the sky seems to be blue – space itself has no color.

In fact, in the *Abhidharma* there is a specific term to refer to the blue sky which is "ornamental space" as it is an object of visual perception. In addition, we can think of space as having a shape, as being a certain aperture that is governed by the shape of what it is within. For example, we can think of square space as in a square hole. But in fact, we are talking about space itself, which has no shape just as it has no color.

The second line says: "Just as space is therefore unaffected or unchanged and unobscured by the various colors and shapes that occur within it," (and is changeless in that it is not composite). So that is the image, the first lines are the image. The third line goes on, "In the same way the essence of your mind transcends color and shape."

As we have to be specific about what type of space we are talking about, in the same way we have to distinguish between two things one could mean by "mind." When we talk about mind in the context of discussing *conventional truth* or relative truths (Tib. *kundzop*) then we are talking about how we experience our mind as being filled with lots of thoughts, lots of happiness, suffering and so forth – we experience it as inexhaustible confusion. But here we are talking about the nature or essence of the mind, so the mind is discussed in the context of *absolute truth* (Tib. *dondam*). At the ultimate level there are no characteristics; no color and shape to the mind, nothing that would indicate any kind of solidity or true existence. While we tend to regard our mind as though it is truly existent, within samadhi – when we directly experience the awareness – there is no solidity, no color, no shape and so forth to mind.

When using inferential reasoning as the path – whether it is the Rangtong school or the Shentong school – there is a lot of discussion of the conventional and absolute truth. In these explanations it is often said that conventional truth is what is experienced within confusion and absolute truth is what is experienced without confusion.

But in the Mahamudra tradition, with the pointing out directly of the view of Mahamudra, there is not much discussion of conventional and absolute truth. While it is true that absolute truth is not the field of conduct of conceptual mind, nevertheless emphasizing the fact that conventional truth is the experience of confusion makes absolute truth sound like it is something that is too far away and cannot be directly experienced. The purpose here is the direct experience of that nature as the nature of one's own mind. For that reason, these terms are not much used for example in this text. What is being discussed here is that when you experience the nature of your own mind, it is in itself, in its own nature, something that is extraordinarily peaceful, extraordinarily pleasant and blissful.

Generally, we talk about the fact that virtuous actions produce states of happiness and harmful actions produce states of misery. When we experience the mind's nature, we find it possesses an inherent peace or blissfulness that transcends the temporary experiences of happiness or suffering produced as a result of our actions. Based on this experience, because of this total peace, there is no need to hope for temporary states of pleasure produced by virtuous actions, and there is no need to fear temporary states or circumstances of suffering produced by negative actions. And that is why in the text it says: "This mind in its nature will never be stained by virtuous and non-virtuous actions, just as the sky is never stained by colors such as white, black and so forth."

This ultimate peace is referred to in the refuge ordinations when one goes to refuge to the dharma and says, "I go for refuge to the dharma, the supreme peace and passionlessness." Generally, we use the word "passion" to sometimes specifically mean desire and sometimes all forms of mental affliction and indeed all forms of deluded experience. Here it is being used in its larger sense, so that ultimate peace – which is experienced as the nature of the mind – is beyond the vicissitudes of circumstances produced by karma.

5. Sunlight as Mind Being Empty and Also Luminosity

The next stanza contains the fifth point concerning the view and is primarily concerned with pointing out the fact that the nature of the mind is not just empty but is at the same time clarity or lucidity. The primary image used in this stanza is the sun.

In the presentation of the Rangtong school, which is primarily an explanation of the second turning of the wheel of dharma connected with the Prajnaparamita, there is a great emphasis on the aspect of emptiness, in particular, the fact that all things are inherently empty. The reason for this emphasis in that context is that generally speaking the biggest or initial karma we have is a fixation on the apparent reality of things; we think that this "self" that I take myself to be is real, these "things" are real. Through taking the self to be real and taking experiences and objects to be real and so forth, we fail to experience "the nature of things" or dharmata. Failing to do so, we do not abandon or transcend obscurations and consequently remain in samsara. To remedy that fixation, emptiness is presented and emphasized, such as the sixteen-fold emptiness, the fourteen-fold emptiness and so forth. In the same way, in the context of this text, the images presented above of the sky, mist and so forth were primarily concerned with remedying this fixation as we apply it to our minds. We normally think, "My mind truly exists. My mind is solid," and that has to be remedied first.

Initially, it is appropriate to emphasize or present emptiness solely as a remedy for fixation on appearances and solidity. However, if it is asked, "Are things merely empty?" The answer would be "no." This is talked about in the sutra tradition, for example when Nagarjuna said, "If someone of prajna comes to be mistaken about emptiness, they accomplish no growing." In the tantric tradition Saraha said, "Those fixated on apparent solidity are like cattle. Those fixated on an absence of solidity are even dumber." What this refers to is the fact that while it is true that the essence or essential nature of all things is emptiness, the essential nature itself is not just empty – it is natural clarity.[25] And this is what has been talked about in this stanza where it says,

> *For example, it is like the luminous heart of the sun, which could never be obscured even by the darkness of a thousand eons. In that way, that luminous clarity that is the essence of the mind is never obscured by the samsara of innumerable kalpas.*

The point of the first two lines don't require much explanation. The third and fourth lines refer to the fact that the inherent brilliance or clarity of the mind itself is never in itself affected by the samsara that occurs around it. Samsara in this case refers to one's own obscurations, the obscurations of the knowable, ignorance, and the obscuration which is mental affliction and so forth. While one is obscured by these, the obscurations – as obscuring as they are – do not affect the nature that they obscure, and that nature is an inherent clarity as well as essential emptiness.

With regard to this aspect of the mind's nature, which is called "luminosity" or "clear light" or "clarity," people often find it harder to recognize luminosity than the mind's essential emptiness. The reason it is harder to recognize is not that it is really harder or more subtle. It is because it is the basic ground of all experience; it is always there, we are used to it so much that we don't really trust that what we are always experiencing could be this clarity. When we are told that the nature of the mind is this inherent luminosity or clarity, we don't believe that this could be referring to the basic cognitive clarity which is what we experience our mind to be. We expect it to be more brilliant, like an electric light or a flame of a candle. But clear light or luminosity or lucidity here refers simply to the inherent capacity of a mind to experience, to experience appearances, and to have cognition. It is true, however, that if this capacity is increased through practice, it does develop into the twofold wisdom of a Buddha – the wisdom of the nature of phenomena and the wisdom of the variety of phenomena

In *The Aspirational Prayer of Mahamudra* by the Third Karmapa, Rangjung Dorje, it says, "The ground of purification is the mind in itself, which is the unity of emptiness and luminosity." The ground of purification here refers not to that which is to be purified but to that nature which is continuous. The unity of luminosity and emptiness here means that the nature of emptiness is luminosity and the nature of luminosity is emptiness.

The next line of the Karmapa's verse is, "That which purifies is the vajrayoga of Mahamudra." Vajrayoga of Mahamudra here refers to recognition of that fundamental nature which is the ground, in other words, the recognition of the mind's nature as being a unity of emptiness and luminosity. The third line explains what is to be purified, "That which is to be purified is the adventitious stains of confusion." This refers to all of the things that arise in the mind, both coarse and subtle thoughts and disturbing emotions that arise continually in our experience. In fact, they come from nowhere, abide nowhere and have no solidity; if they are unrecognized, they take hold of us and bind us.

The unity of emptiness and luminosity is also clearly taught in the sutra tradition. While this tradition uses inferential reasoning as its basis, nevertheless the explanations are of such clarity that they can assist our understanding. For example, Mipham Rinpoche wrote that, "This appearance does not lose its vividness as appearance." This means that we constantly experience things, for example, visible forms such as pillars, houses, mountains, gardens and so forth, and yet even while there is this vivid experience, all of this is groundless, rootless from the beginning, without any inherent essence or nature. Then Mipham goes on to say, "This emptiness does not lose its status as emptiness or its being emptiness. Interdependence arises unimpeded." What is being referred to in this quote is that normally when we hear explanations on appearance and emptiness as a unity, we think of these as either contradictory or somehow alternating. We think that there are at least two different things and we tend to imagine them as being one thing empty and another thing appearing, or something appearing sometimes and being empty at other times. But, in fact, it is not like this at all. The fundamental nature is unchanging and yet this in no way obstructs the unimpededness of the interdependent manifestations of this nature. Of course, this is in the language and style of the sutras, but that does not mean that it is not helpful to us in this context.

When we say that the mind is in nature empty, this in no way contradicts the fact that we experience the mind as an unimpeded expression of clarity. And while we experience the visible forms, audible sounds and so forth, this does not in any way obstruct or impede the fact that this mind's nature and the nature of what is experienced are emptiness. And that is what is meant by unity: the aspect of emptiness and the aspect of clarity are neither separate nor mutually obstructive. In this stanza of the song, this is communicated using the image of sunlight.

Up to this point, these various stanzas have described first the emptiness of the mind's nature and then the luminosity of the mind's nature.

6. The Inexpressibility of the Mind's Nature

The sixth stanza of the explanation of the view is concerned with the indescribability or inexpressibility of the mind's nature. The stanza begins:

For example, just as we apply the term empty to space, in fact, there is nothing within space that we are accurately describing by that term. In the same way, although we call the mind clear light or luminosity, simply calling it so does not make it true that there is actually any thing within the mind that is a true basis for that designation.

The point of this verse is essentially that we cannot describe this fundamental nature, what this mind is really like. This means that even when a guru tries to communicate an experience to his students by saying that the mind's nature is the unity of emptiness and clarity, this is just an approximate indication and does not really intend to fully describe what the mind's nature really is.

When we actually experience the mind's nature, we have nothing to say about it because, as it says in the stanza, "There is no basis within it for description, there is no solid, identifiable conceptually graspable quality that we can then describe with words, language and thought." This is also talked about in *The Praise to Prajnaparamita* where it says, "Prajnaparamita is beyond speech, thought and description." In one of the songs of Marpa it says, "An indescribable experience arose and I was like a mute person tasting sugar." This means that even for Marpa, when practicing under the guidance of Naropa and receiving empowerment from him, was not able to communicate this experience in words.

In that way, the nature of the mind has from the beginning been like space, and there are no dharmas that are not included within that.

There are seven main sections or topics to "The Ganges Mahamudra" taught by Tilopa and we have completed the first of the seven, which was the explanation of the view in six points.

Questions

Question: Is the teaching of Buddha-essence a practice that is taught just in the Vajrayana?

Rinpoche: The revelation of Buddha-essence is not particularly Vajrayana because the Buddha taught two types of doctrines, one called "sutra" and the other called "tantra." The basic difference between these two is not the revelation of Buddha-essence but whether the nature of the path is inference – inferential reasoning in the case of sutra – or direct experience in the case of tantra, mantra or Vajrayana. Again, the sutra can be divided into two approaches, the Hinayana ("lesser vehicle") and the Mahayana ("greater vehicle"). The Mahayana itself can be divided into two presentations, what is called "the second turning of the wheel of dharma" (in which the emphasis was on the presentation of the space or emptiness aspect) and "the third turning of the wheel of dharma" (in which the emphasis was on the clarity of the Buddha-essence aspect). There is no real difference in the importance of two aspects of the

Mahayana presentations because both are necessary. Neither approach is entirely sufficient to understand the Mahayana because each type of presentation needs to be augmented by the other. For example, some things that are presented in one view will not be entirely clear, while other things will not be entirely clear in the other approach.

However, a distinction can be made between these two phases of the presentation of Mahayana, in regard to how they are employed. In the context of the second turning of the wheel it is taught how to cut through elaborations or false projections by demonstrating emptiness more clearly. But because it suggests that emptiness remains after these elaborations have been cut through, it is hard to understand from this point of view how we should practice meditation on emptiness. It is easier to practice meditation upon luminosity as presented in the third wheel of dharma. So, in the third turning, which is meditation following upon hearing and thinking, and in the context of traditions where meditation is emphasized, the third turning of the wheel – which is called "the wheel of final distinction or final subtle distinctions" – is emphasized more.

Question: Would Rinpoche give some instruction on a rule of Mahamudra to overcome laziness and to practice more? How do you engender more of that longing and confidence that would inspire us?

Rinpoche: A method which is recommended in this situation for the development of energy or exertion is a way of turning one's trust in the dharma by reflecting on the four thoughts or reminders, and these are (1) the difficulty of acquiring the opportunities and resources of a precious human existence, (2) death and impermanence, (3) the workings of karma and (4) the defects of samsara. So these four could be contemplated, and of these four especially the second, impermanence. It was said by the Buddha that initially impermanence inspires us to begin to practice dharma, and when we are practicing it, it is impermanence which exhorts us to diligence in practice. Then in the end it is impermanence which is the assistant or friend that accompanies awakening, and facilitates enlightenment. So we can study impermanence in texts and contemplate it according to those texts. Or we can take the approach that Milarepa who said in one of his songs, "Everything that appears and exists is a book for me. I have never studied written texts." This means that if you wish to come to a definitive appreciation of impermanence, all you have to do is look around and see situations, the changes constantly occurring around you, what is happening to your friends, what is happening to other people, what is happening to animals; by automatically seeing, you can generate trust in impermanence, trust in dharma, which will exhort you to diligence.

Question: Looking directly at the experience of mind, sometimes you talk about it in other aspects, in terms of looking as the manifestation of appearances. I just wondered, the instructions you talked about above, which is basically looking directly at the mind in terms of thoughts, I wondered if that is preferable?

Rinpoche: Well, when you are trying to go through the process of hearing and thinking, that is establishing a type of knowledge in order to cut through elaborations or misconceptions or misapprehensions. In that context, distinctions are made between the cognitive clarity aspect of mind and the appearance or experience aspect of mind and so forth, between the eight consciousnesses; between mind and what arises in it. Here in this approach there are no real divisions. When you look directly at your mind, then there is a clarity or lucidity or you could say there is emptiness. Basically, you are experiencing nothing at all, so you could say it is just empty or just clarity. But there is certainly no emphasis placed in this context on distinguishing between the aspect of appearances and the aspect of clarity.

8

The Conduct of Mahamudra

Now we are beginning the second of the seven sections, which is an explanation of the conduct.[26]

The Conduct of Actual Meditation

Abandoning all physical actions, the practitioner should rest at ease. Without any verbal utterance, your speech becomes like an echo, sound inseparable from emptiness. Think of nothing whatsoever with the mind and look at the dharmas of the leap.

These three lines are concerned with the conduct of actual meditation practice and the lines which follow will be concerned with post-meditation conduct.

The first of these three lines deals with correct use of the body: "Abandoning all physical actions, the practitioner should rest at ease." In the practice of meditation it is necessary to sit in the manner that is physically still, not tense but natural and relaxed. In the narrow sense, this can refer to the posture called the *seven dharmas of Vairochana* or to whatever sitting posture used, but the key point is naturalness and relaxation.

When we meditate, we have the tendency to try to tighten or crank up our awareness and this causes our channels, muscles and so forth to tighten as well. Because we tend to do this in practice, people complain, saying, "When I meditate, I get exhausted. When I meditate, it simply hurts." All this happens from tightening up too much, so in the sitting posture we should be extremely relaxed so that our muscles, joints, and bones actually start to relax. Otherwise, when we meditate we may feel as though our heart or brain were being squeezed or bound in some way. This point was explained by Machig Labchi Drolma when speaking of meditation posture. She said, "The essential point of physical posture is that the channels and muscles of the limbs be relaxed."

Sometimes, even though we may consciously relax our entire body while meditating, we still exert some tension with our eyes, and this will cause them to water while practicing. We are not to blame for becoming tense in this way, but nevertheless it is necessary to learn to overcome this. Once we have taken the posture – whether the seven dharmas of Vairochana or the fivefold posture[27] of meditation – properly, we should relax while remaining in that posture and not try to maintain it through physical tension. In a similar way, when meditating some people try to control their breathing. It is important in the context of this practice to just let the breath be totally natural, breathing the way we always breathe, so if the breath is long, don't try to shorten it; if it is short, don't try to lengthen it. It is important in this way to put some attention into conscious relaxation of our body, of our eyes and our breathing when we begin to meditate.

The second line says, "Without any verbal utterance, your speech becomes like an echo, sound inseparable from emptiness." This line refers to meditation practice. In post-meditation it is fine to speak. Speech in meditation is to be considered to be like an echo, which means that past utterances are finished, gone and done with and not to be thought about. So speech in the context of the formal practice of meditation should be seen as irrelevant, of no more consequence than an echo.

This is important because the main cause of distracting thoughts in meditation is not the external forms with which we come into contact but the tendency to talk to ourselves internally. This internal conversation is usually concerned with what we have said and done in the past and with what we will say and do in the future. It is this internal speech that is to be seen of as no more consequence than an echo, and as of the nature of the unity of sound and emptiness.

In fact, two things are being referred to in this line: One is to actually view the sounds which might actually disturb us, the sounds which you hear in meditation as like an echo, and also to view the internal conversation that arises as a distraction as an echo, and not to follow after them, and in that way not to be distracted by them.

The third line refers to the actual conduct of the mind during meditation: "Think of nothing whatsoever with the mind and look at the dharmas of the leap." "Don't think" here could be misinterpreted in many different ways. It does not literally mean trying not to think; it means to not fixate on and to have no attachment for whatever thoughts arise. We do this so we don't try to prolong them. The key term used in this line is the Tibetan *lha-da*, literally "to get beyond the pass." I suggest that it could be translated as "leap" or *trong-wa*. The point of leap here is an aspect of that which distinguishes between the Mahamudra approach and the approach using inferential reasoning. If we are attempting to use inferential reasoning to uncover the ultimate nature of absolute truth, then there is no leap involved, because the process consists of considering what there is and gradually generating confidence in its ultimate nature as absolute truth. In the Mahamudra approach, however, there is a leap. What we are leaping past is conceptual consideration altogether, and what we are leaping into is the direct experience of the nature of our own mind. So, there is no consideration or analysis or labeling of substantiality, insubstantiality and so forth – we are simply directly looking at the nature of our mind, directly experiencing it, and thereby directly meditating upon it.

Now, the essence or nature of mind is being essentially empty, luminous in nature and of an unimpeded variety of manifestations. Yet while we experience this, we can say that while we are looking at the essential emptiness, we are not labeling it, or thinking, "Oh, this is empty, this is the clarity" and so forth. Of course, it is emptiness, but we are not labeling it. Rather we just experience the nature of the mind without attempting to draw any inferences from it.

Post-Meditation Conduct

The next three lines are concerned with post-meditation. The first of the three reads:

The body is without meaning, empty like a bamboo stalk.

While we are usually greatly attached to our bodies, in fact our bodies are without essence, which means that they have no true existence and are not true units; they are composites without true existence. The image used here to communicate that lack of essence of a body is a hollow bamboo tube or bamboo stock. The second line says:

The mind is like the midst of space. It is inconceivable.

Here again the image for the mind is space. "The midst of the sky or the midst of space" refers to the fact that if you look at the horizon, you will see many things, but if you look into the very center of the sky, you won't see anything. It says the mind's nature is like that. Of course, if you look at the content of thoughts, one after another, there will be no end to the possible examination of the contents of those thoughts. But the mind itself cannot be seen or examined. For example in *The Aspirational Prayer of Mahamudra* by the Third Karmapa, Rangjung Dorje he says: "It does not exist nor does it not-exist. It is not even seen by the Victorious Ones. It is the basis of all samsara and nirvana. This is not a contradiction – it is the Middle-way. May I realize the dharmata of the mind which is beyond these extremes."

Normally if we say that something does not exist we would say it must not exist. Or if something does not not-exist, it must exist. To say that something is both is considered a logical contradiction. But what is being said here about the mind's nature is that we cannot say that it exists, we also cannot say that it does not-exist, and it is untrue that there is a contradiction between these two statements.

The Conduct of Mahamudra

The fourth line of Rangjung Dorje's spiritual song says, "May I realize the dharmata of the mind which is beyond these extremes." "Beyond extremes" here means it does not fall into either extreme of existence or non-existence. There is a nearly identical verse from the Dzogchen tradition composed by the Omniscient Drimed Lingpa, which says exactly the same thing in the first three lines. The third line concludes, "It transcends utterance or cannot be described. May this nature of the ground great perfection be realized." The point is that in either tradition, Mahamudra or Dzogchen, the nature of the mind is understood in the same way.

The third line of Tilopa's song goes on to say:

Rest relaxed within that, without letting it go or placing it. Rest relaxed in that state without sending it out or placing it in, letting it go or attempting to place it.

What is indicated here is that in the practice of Mahamudra one makes no attempt to either generate or create mental activities or contents of mind, nor to intentionally or forcefully exclude or get rid of contents; to force the mind to sit still. In other words, it is not a question of squeezing or pressing the mind into shape; it is rather a matter of relaxing.

Those lines were an explanation of the conduct of Mahamudra.

Questions

Question: Kalu Rinpoche used to speak about the nature of mind as being empty, clear, and unimpeded. I was wondering if you could say something about what unimpeded means. It is *mang gakpa* in Tibetan and I never really understood that.

Rinpoche: *Mang gakpa,* the unceasing manifestation of the mind, is an aspect of lucidity. If you describe the mind using the two concepts, emptiness and cognitive lucidity, then that would include the aspect of unceasing manifestation or unimpededness. But in more detail, you can say that the mind is empty of essence, naturally lucid, and of unceasing manifestation. It is easiest to explain this by going back to the emptiness of the mind. As you know, the mind is called empty because when you look for it, it is not there to be found. It has no substantial characteristics, and it has no substantial existence. When we try to embrace this conceptually – this not having any substantiality – we generate a concept of nothingness or nothing or non-existence. If the mind were nothing, then you would not be alive. Your body would be inert matter. So while it is true to say that the mind is empty in the sense that it has nothing substantial within it or that nothing substantial can be found, it nevertheless never stops. The fundamental meaning of *mang gakpa* is that while there is nothing there that never stops, it never stops. It never stops in the sense that you can think, you can remember, you continue to experience. What it is that never stops, if you have to give it a name, it is the lucidity. It is the unimpededness or unceasing quality of the lucidity itself. Therefore, it is usually called the unceasing manifestation – *nangpa mang gakpa* – or the unceasing gleam or display or image.

Question: Rinpoche, with the idea of leap, "to get beyond the pass" as you mentioned. What enables one to avoid the long path of going around and what enables one to actually have the capability of leaping over? Because in the stories of Naropa and Milarepa it seems that before they actually realized the nature of mind, each one of them underwent tremendous difficulties. Do we need in modern culture to undergo similar hardships? Is this somehow a preparation for us to leap over?

Rinpoche: A distinction needs to be made between the simple recognition of the mind's nature and the full revelation or realization of the mind's nature. In order to recognize the nature of your mind, heroic austerities like those of Jetsun Milarepa are not necessary. But in order to fully realize the nature of your mind they might be. For example, when Jetsun Milarepa first received instruction from Marpa, he instantly recognized the nature of his mind because that is what Marpa was explaining to him, and Milarepa understood it. But all of his subsequent austerities and practice were undergone in order to realize fully what he had already recognized.[28] As for how necessary such austerities are in the present day, well if you can engage in that degree of austerity, then of course that is the very best, because the result will be very quick and the result will be indeed extraordinary in other ways. But you should not think that the success or failure of your practice is based upon your ability or inability to do what Milarepa did. Because any degree of realization of the mind's nature will make your practice and your life completely worthwhile and meaningful. If you can generate one hundred percent of the realization of Milarepa, of course, that would be magnificent. But even fifty percent or twenty-five percent or ten percent or five percent or even one percent would still be extraordinary. You should not think that you are in some way disqualified as a practitioner merely because you cannot equal the example of Jetsun Milarepa. Any amount of Mahamudra practice you do will be strongly beneficial.

Question: Rinpoche, I am wondering about *chöd* practice. I am thinking about the various demons and hindrances that are discussed in chöd practice as they relate to the realization of Mahamudra. I am wondering if you could explain a little bit what some of those hindrances are that we might encounter in our practice. For example, could you explain further the demon or hindrance of blocking or solidity?

Translator: Blocking or solidity – is that one of the four talked about in chöd, is it *top che dup*? And exactly what are you asking about it? Why does it happen, or how do we deal with it?

Question: Yes. Both.

Rinpoche: First of all, chöd is Mahamudra. Chöd is a style or tradition of Mahamudra practice. In fact, the name of it is *chödyul chakgya chenpo*, chöd Mahamudra. Chöd is a way of practicing or implementing the Mahamudra view. What we normally refer to as chöd practice is the enhancement of the view of Mahamudra by using that which inspires fear or kleshas. You are working with situations that cause internal kleshas, or cause you to be afraid of external things, such as spirits and so forth. You are learning to cut through your fear and your conceptualization about those situations. If you can cut through those most stressful situations, then you can rest in the recognition of your mind's nature under all circumstances. The point of chöd practice is to widen and deepen your recognition of Mahamudra or the nature of the mind.

Four *maras* are talked about in the chöd tradition: the substantial mara, the insubstantial mara, the mara of arrogance, and the mara of delight. The substantial mara is present when because of various circumstances, specifically the presence of kleshas within you and various conditions such as certain energies moving within the channels, you perceive externally something that you would identify as a mara, as an external manifestation which appears to be external to you and to be substantial and separate from you. It is therefore called the substantial mara. The key point in working with this is to understand that you do not see these things when your mind is at rest. You see them when your mind is agitated through an imbalance of the elements or other similar conditions. The way to relate to the maras is simply to cut through any kind of conceptualization of their inherent and separate existence. You recognize that they are simply the natural manifestation of your own internal being and processes. In that way, through experiencing them and cutting through fixation on their existence, you come to a further recognition of dharmata.

Question: Rinpoche, could you say more about the conduct of speech?

Rinpoche: The main point in the presentation of the conduct of speech here is that, because Mahamudra is the path of liberation, there is not anything to be chanted or practiced verbally. The practice of speech connected with Mahamudra is basically silence. Connected with that is perceiving sound or relating to sound as insubstantial like an echo or like the unity of sound and emptiness. The point of this whole section is the same for body, speech, and mind. Whether you are talking about the body, about speech, or about the mind, the essence of Mahamudra is that there is no special effort involved. This does not mean that if you are practicing Mahamudra you must abandon the recitation of mantras, or that it is forbidden for a Mahamudra practitioner to recite mantras, or that if you are a Mahamudra practitioner that you must cease working, or that it is forbidden for a Mahamudra practitioner to move. It does not mean this. It means that there is no specific form of physical activity and no specific form of verbal activity, such as the recitation of mantra or liturgy or ritual that is required for Mahamudra practice.

Question: But what Rinpoche said about insubstantiality .. [further clarification of previous question]

Rinpoche: The section of the line that says, ".. like an echo, sound inseparable from emptiness," is explaining the reason for this approach to speech in Mahamudra. The reason why no particular speech is regarded as necessary or more important than another, is that speech and sound are just emptiness arising as sound. They are just one of the expressions of emptiness. In that sense they are like an echo. They are not something real. They are just something that you are experiencing. So therefore, whatever speech arises has that same fundamental quality or same fundamental nature, and therefore does not especially need to be cultivated.

Question: Rinpoche, could you say something about where devotion comes into Mahamudra; what the relationship is between Mahamudra and devotion?

Rinpoche: Devotion has two functions in the practice of Mahamudra. One of them you could think of as an immediate function or immediate benefit of devotion, and the other one is the main or true function of devotion. The immediate function is that sometimes when you supplicate the root and lineage gurus with intense devotion, your perception, your outlook, changes completely. In an instant there is a great change in how you experience the world, and the result is that on the spot there will be considerable progress. For example, if up to then you had had no experience or recognition of your mind's nature, then you might have that experience and whatever recognition and experience you have had will increase. So that is kind of an immediate or short-term benefit of devotion, which is simply that devotion brings blessings, and blessings bring progress. But the true function of devotion is even simpler or more basic than that. It is that the more trust and the more interest and confidence you have in something, the more you will put into it. To the extent that you trust Mahamudra, that you are interested in Mahamudra, that you regard it as authentic and trustworthy, to that extent you will actually engage in practicing it. If you lack devotion, which means, if you are suspicious of Mahamudra, if you think, "How could it be so easy, how could this actually work – something so simple as this?" If you think that, if you think there is something a little fishy about it and you do not trust it, obviously you are not going to practice it. When someone takes that attitude of suspicion, no matter how many times Mahamudra is taught to them and no matter how much instruction they receive, obviously it is not going to do them any good, because they do not buy it. If you have one hundred percent confidence, and here devotion is the same as confidence, if you have one hundred percent confidence in Mahamudra, you will have one hundred percent diligence. If you have fifty percent confidence, you will have fifty percent diligence. Here, we are talking about Mahamudra, but this function of devotion is actually common to all endeavors, whether spiritual or mundane. The more confidence you have in something, the more you will put into it and the more you will get out of it.

9

The Meditation of Mahamudra

The next section is an explanation of the meditation of Mahamudra.
This is the third section of this text, which begins:

If mind has no direction, it is Mahamudra. With this you will attain unsurpassable awakening.

The word *te-so* means an "object, target or reference." This means that if you are without consideration of something, thinking, "This exists, or this doesn't exist" and so forth, if you are without that confusion which is the arising of the sixth consciousness, the mental consciousness and its attendant confusion, if you are without that, then you will remain in the state of direct experience. And it is this state of direct experience which is possible when the mind is not directed at something in particular, that is needed here. Beyond that, when one has begun to cultivate this practice, one cannot just simply let it go, but one has to keep on working with it. This is referred to here as "becoming facilitated in and becoming used to," which means one applies this point of direct experience in both meditation and post-meditation training. If you do this, then this will lead to supreme awakening. Cultivation consists of these two aspects, the experience of the leap in meditation and of recognition in post-meditation.

Continuing with the section on meditation, now the method of the practice of Mahamudra has been given. Next is an explanation of what isn't Mahamudra or how fixation on a view will not lead to Mahamudra. This is true irrespective of the sophistication or height of the view. And it says in the text:

Those who follow tantra and the vehicle of the paramitas, the Vinaya, the Sutras, and the various teachings of the Buddha with an attachment for their individual textual traditions and their individual philosophy will not come to see luminous Mahamudra.

When it says, "Those who follow tantra," it means people who are involved in Vajrayana without this essential point of Mahamudra. In other words, the Vajrayana without Mahamudra will not work. In the same way, while the practice of the Mahayana discipline of the *paramitas* could be combined with Mahamudra and lead to realization of that, if this essential element is missing, it will also not lead to the realization of Mahamudra, neither will the other disciplines of dharma which are enumerated. The point is: As long as one's view remains conceptual, no matter what it is, it is not Mahamudra and will not enable you to experience or realize Mahamudra.

So, the first two lines in the section on meditation explained the method of meditation itself. Then the next two lines were concerned with what will not lead to realization of Mahamudra, in other words, how attempts to practice without this essential point will not work.

Having been asserted that without this essential point all other conceptual views will not produce realization, the next line explains why. It reads:

Because the seeing of that luminosity or clear light is obscured by their intention and attitude.

"Intention and attitude" here refers to the fact that any conceptual view is cultivated by intellect or conceptual mind. And the intellect is a function of confusion and therefore of ignorance. So, in fact, a conceptual view – regardless of how sophisticated it may seem to be – is a direct obscuration in itself of the mind's nature and prevents one from seeing it directly. So, that which obscures the nature of the mind, that which prevents one from experiencing it directly (in the case of someone who has a conceptual view) is the fact that this view is conceptual, that it is an assertion that is made with intellectual fixation. So, whatever practice one does, it is necessary that there be the experience of no reference point or no target or object in the mind and that there be a direct experience rather than a conceptual or inferential evaluation, that there be a direct experience of the mind's nature. Otherwise, whatever the practice is, it will not produce the realization of Mahamudra.

Questions

Question: Rinpoche, when you were talking about the aspects of the mind, one is unimpededness or unobstructiveness, and I wondered if it would be all right to think that this is in terms of impermanence, rather than things being followed, whether they were thoughts or sounds, and so not allowing something else to arise? Being impermanent, they pass on and therefore things arise. Is that all right?

Rinpoche: Actually the idea of unceasing variety or unceasing display refers more to permanence and continuity than it does to impermanence. The connotation of the term is "permanence, something that is unceasing, that does not cease and therefore is permanent." What it refers to is a quality of the mind's nature. Of course, the four cardinal doctrines or dogmas of Buddhism, which are called "the *four seals* of the view or authorized fields of the view," include the one which is that all composites are impermanent. Therefore, if you accept any composite thing to be permanent, it is a non-Buddhist view.

What is being asserted here when it is said that "The nature of the mind possesses the manifestation that is unceasing" is not the solidity of something composite but the fact that because the mind's nature has no true existence as one thing or another, it is unceasing because it does not arise and therefore does not cease and so forth. However, a thought itself or a thing itself is not unceasing because it does appear to arise and to cease. For example, thoughts are manifestations of cognition or of cognitive experience, cognitive clarity. And that particular manifestation of cognitive clarity which is a particular thought does arise and does cease. So a thought would not be considered unceasing. But the nature of the mind in which and for which the thought arises is unceasing, in the sense that it transcends the *four extremes* and elaborations. Therefore, its manner, its very emptiness, is experienced as an unceasing variety. So, in fact, it refers more to permanence and continuity and an unchanging quality that nevertheless is totally devoid of any kind of solidity.

Question: You said that we must keep on working on experiencing this direct experience of mind, both in meditation and post-meditation and become used to it. This is what I wasn't clear about: that cultivation is the experience of leap in meditation practice and recognition in post-meditation practice. I think you explained the idea of leap, but I wondered more about cultivating recognition in practice?

Rinpoche: The distinction made between the experience of the leap in meditation or even-placement and the use of recognition in post-meditation is that meditation or even-placement being just that, there isn't a great deal of thought that arises, so it is a practice that is not concerned with the recognition of thought but simply with experiencing this fundamental nature. However, in post-meditation, because one is active, thoughts do arise and therefore the practice manifests more in post-meditation as attempting to experience what arises within a continued recognition of this fundamental nature of Mahamudra. And one is fostering or trying to continue the experience of this nature in the post-meditation, but it is distinct from meditation in that there is activity and therefore thought. So these two aspects of practice assist each other; meditation enhances post-meditation and vice versa.

Question: I wondered if you would clarify that mind itself cannot be seen or examined. Previously you said that one has to look directly into mind, where mind looks at itself.

Rinpoche: Well, these types of statements are literally contradictory and this happens a lot. Sometimes a text will say, "See your mind" and the next moment it will say, "You can't see your mind." Or it will say, "The mind looks at the mind,"[29] which transcends being viewed" and so forth. The reason for these kinds of contradictory statements and contradictory directives and instructions is that the nature of the mind and how it is experienced cannot be truly indicated by any words — we can't say the mind exists, nor can we say it doesn't, we can't say you can look at it and we can't say you can't, but none of these things are a really true or accurate description of the mind's nature or the experience of it. However, at the same time, while we can't really say anything about it, we can't just say nothing because then there would be no explanation, no communication. So, although on a practical level it is contradictory to do so, we do need to give instruction or a direction, and therefore we say things like, "Do this and don't do that when you meditate" and so forth.

So, in some contexts we say that the mind's nature is seen, but it doesn't mean literally seen. For example, if I look at the vajra and bell on the table in front of me, I can literally see them and you can see them as well, but we cannot see the nature of our minds in this same literal way. However, there has to be some way of communicating what we are trying to talk about.

At the same time, while the mind's nature is beyond thought and beyond description, it is not impossible to realize, and the realization of it does lead to the awakening of a Buddha. As we can see, siddhas of the past have realized it and we are meditating upon it now and we will realize it and so we will also attain awakening. So, while it is impossible to talk about it in the fullest sense, it is incorrect to therefore take the attitude, "Well, no one has ever seen this. I might as well forget it." While there appear to be contradictory statements on a practical level, they are not contradictory.[30]

Question: When you talk about the nature of the mind, are you also referring to the essence of the mind?

Rinpoche: Well, these terms *no-wo* or "essence" and *nam-jen* or "nature" and *nae-lug* or "manner of abiding" can be used distinctly in this context and are really referring to the same thing, which you can call "essence, nature or manner of abiding."

Fundamentally what is being referred to as the essence or nature of the mind here is what can also be called "the direct or naked nature of the mind." One way it can be explained is that normally in a confused state we are involved with an apparent solidity of experience of our mind because there is a thought that has just ceased and we jump from the thought that just ceased to the next thought that is just about to begin. And we jump from thought to thought experiencing apparent solidity because of the continuity of the passage of thoughts from past to future. But if we rest directly in the present instant or present moment, then with the in-between of what has just finished and not yet begun we can experience that, whereas thoughts may arise and cease, the mind itself has not come from anywhere, isn't anywhere now and isn't going anywhere. In that sense, it is like space, except that it isn't merely like space because at the same time there is a cognitive clarity, a cognitive lucidity. However, while you can say this, while you try to figure this out or conceptualize it or say, "It is really like this" – like anything you can say about it – then you run into the problem explained in the text, "Assertion with fixation obscures this nature." On the other hand, if you meditate and experience this directly, as you meditate you can experience this directly. This is more or less what we mean when we talk about essence or nature of the mind.

10

The Samaya of Mahamudra

The fourth of the seven main topics of the text concerns the samaya or commitments of Mahamudra. It begins with the words:

The conceptualized maintenance of vows actually causes you to impair the meaning of samaya. Without mental directedness or mental activity, be free of all intentionality. Thoughts are self-arisen and self-pacified like designs on the surface of water. If you do not pass beyond the meaning which is not abiding and not conceptualizing or focusing, then through not passing beyond that, you do not pass beyond or transgress samaya.

The Sanskrit word "samaya" was translated by all Tibetan translators into Tibetan as *dam-zig*. The first syllable *dam* means "a promise, a commitment, an undertaking," the thought or the acknowledgment, "I will do such and such." The second syllable *zig*, which is often taken to mean "word," here actually means "a joint juncture, border or boundary," like the joints in a bamboo tube which are called *zig*. What it means here is "that which is not to be passed beyond," like a limit or a border or a boundary.

Sometimes samaya is misunderstood and people consider it to be some undertaking we make at the time of empowerment. For example, people often think that they are under a constraint by samaya to recite certain mantras associated with empowerments they have received at least a hundred times a day, and if they miss a day, then something terrible will happen, their samaya will be broken and they will fall into the *lower realms*. Of course, it is good if you commit yourself to doing such a thing, but not doing it is not what is meant by breaking samaya. Some people think that samaya is something terribly delicate and dangerous and that if you make the slightest mistakes with regard to the formalities of your commitments, you will plunge head-long into the lower realms. This is not exactly true. At the same time, if you ask whether samaya is something unimportant that we can ignore, this is absolutely not true either. What we need, finally, is to be liberated, and liberation can only come from practice and practice can only come from diligence or exertion. So a commitment, a personal commitment, to practice is essential, and the thought, "I will do this much practice. I will follow the instructions or commands of my *root guru*" and so forth – these personal commitments are very important. If these commitments are present, if you are committed to practice on the path, then the practice will produce a result, which is liberation. And if you don't fulfill your commitment, then obviously having said you would, the words of promise – whatever ritual you went through – are meaningless. But, it is not the case that a failure to fulfill these commitments immediately places you in the category of a samaya-breaker who will plunge head-long into the lower realms. Nevertheless, it is important to fulfill or follow up on the commitments you make to practice.

Now, the specific context in which samaya is being discussed here is of the view and meditation of Mahamudra. The first line in the first statement is: "The conceptualized maintenance of vows actually causes you to impair the meaning of samaya."

On a practical level, on the level of *kundzop* or "relative truth," it is obviously necessary to put some attention into behaving properly and not allowing oneself to get involved with conduct that is inferior, which means harmful, and in non-virtuous actions of any kind, and this is necessary and very good. This type of mindfulness and attentiveness is, of course, important; it is important not to be degenerate. But at the same time, while this is true, at the same time, the concept, "I am keeping these rules. I am doing this. I will do this. I will not do that" and so forth, the concept and fixation upon that concept does obstruct even-placement or meditation of Mahamudra because it is a fiercely held concept. So in that sense, if there is a conceptual fixation on one's moral choices, this in a sense is contradictory to the samaya of absolute truth, which is the samaya of Mahamudra.

The samaya of Mahamudra is not a matter of the intention, or not to do something; it is not kept by thinking, "I will do this and I will not do that." It is defined in the next line i.e. a state without desire or without attachment: "Without mental directedness or mental activity,.."
When it says "without mental directedness," it means without the conceptual fixation on solidity or the absence of solidity; the existence or the absence of existence. The samaya of Mahamudra is fostering the experience of the mind's nature, just allowing that to be experienced rather than attempting to create a conceptualized experience.

While one is doing this, while one is practicing in this way, of course thoughts arise, and this is discussed in the next line: "Thoughts are self-arisen and self-pacified like designs on the surface of water." What this means is that thoughts which seem to just arise of themselves in the same way do disappear and do not need to be chased out or intentionally gotten rid of. The image given in the line is a design that is written in water, which will surely vanish, perhaps even before the design is finished. Because thoughts are nothing other than the unimpeded or unceasing display of the mind, there is no need to attempt to get rid of them and there is no need to view them as obstacles. So, thoughts are not considered to be something that need to be intentionally abandoned.

The next line says: "If you do not pass beyond the meaning which is not abiding and not conceptualizing or focusing, then through not passing beyond that, you do not pass beyond or transgress samaya."
The three points in this line refer to how one practices within the samaya of Mahamudra.

Generally we think that meditation consists of the mind staying still, the mind abiding or being at rest, and while there is an experience of stillness, nevertheless the mind is not actually at rest because there is no place, we can't say that it abides anywhere, and also the mind itself isn't a thing that can abide, so there is no abider or abiding. If there is an experience of the mind being still somewhere, then that is conceptual and not direct experience.

The second point *mi-mig-pa* ("without a reference") means that in the practice of Mahamudra there is no object or objective reference to the meditation and there is no truly existent cognition that could have such an object, so there is no reference-point whatsoever. The third point "not departing from the meaning" means that while one may think that because this is a state without anything abiding anywhere and without any reference-point, it must be just nothing, a nothingness – this is not true. The meaning that is referred to here is recognition of the mind's nature, and "not departing from that and not transcending that," means not wandering or straying from recognition of the mind's nature. This means that while one does not intentionally attempt to get rid of thoughts, one does not allow oneself to be controlled by them; one doesn't let them run wild – one maintains awareness or recognition of the mind's nature.

These three points are the samayas of what is to be done, what is to be accomplished, and the previous samayas about not trying to get rid of thoughts and so forth are samayas about what is not to be done. So, if these points are maintained, then this is the keeping of pure and genuine samaya without violation. Therefore the next line which finishes the previous one in the text says:

This is the torch which dispels all obscurity or darkness. If free of all intention you do not abide in extremes, you will see without exception the meaning of all the Buddha's teachings or of all the sections of the Buddha's teachings.

Now, with regard to being free of extremes, in the *Uttaratantra* and some other tantras as well it says, "There is nothing here to be removed, nothing here to be added. By genuinely or perfectly looking at that which is genuine or perfect, you will become genuinely or perfectly awakened." Of course, on a conventional level we can say that there is a great deal to be removed and possibly something to be added. But the point is that there is nothing to be removed and nothing that need or could be added to the nature of the mind. What this means is that the correct or genuine way to experience this nature is to be without any attempt to reify or conceptualize it as being existent or as being non-existent, to being without any investment in a conceptual evaluation of it. If you remain without such an investment in a conceptual view of the mind, then you will see the essence of all dharmas, of the three baskets (Skt. *pithaka*). The reason is that simply remaining in this state that does not fall into either extreme of existence or non-existence is pure samaya, and is at the same time the result of and shows the necessity of pure samaya.

All the dharmas of the three baskets of the teachings are all the teachings given by the Buddha: the Vinaya-pithaka (or "the basket of discipline"), which presents the superior training in discipline), the Sutra-pithaka (or "basket of discourses"), which presents the training in samadhi (or "meditative absorption"), and the Abhidharma-pithaka (or "basket of Abhidharma"), which presents training in knowledge or understanding. They can also be considered from the point of view of what they emphasize as their target or what they remedy. Generally speaking, it is said that the Buddha gave 21,000 teachings on discipline connected with the Vinaya as a remedy for the disturbing emotion of attachment, 21,000 teachings on meditation presented in the sutras as a remedy for aggression, 21,000 teachings of Abhidharma as a remedy for mental dullness, and 21,000 teachings which were aimed at dealing with all three disturbing emotions at once, and this probably refers to the tantras.

So there are said to be 84.000 different types of teachings given by the Buddha, and obviously if you had to know or even see all of these, you would be in a very difficult position. However, the way that dharma works is that fully understanding any one aspect of it leads to liberation or a full unleashing of the meaning of all of it, and that is what is being pointed out here: If there is a general understanding or recognition of the nature of the mind which transcends the extremes of existence and non-existence, then within that recognition there is seeing the essence of all the teachings of the Buddha.

11

The Benefits of Practicing Mahamudra

If you rest in this, you will be liberated from the prison of samsara.

The first line deals with the removal of the effect which is samsara, and the following line deals with the removal of the cause, which is wrong-doing and obscurations. What these lines are saying is: If you realize this view, practice this meditation, abide within this conduct and observe these samayas, then you will be liberated.

Normally, whatever we undergo – whether suffering or happiness, abiding in a lower or *higher realm* – is all samsara. Regardless of how pleasant or unpleasant it may be, its fundamental nature is the same in that it is like a prison, it is a self-contained situation from which one cannot escape. Because our minds are driven by thought, by conceptuality, and because of the shackles of thought, we cannot let go of our obscurations, we cannot expand our qualities, we mistake that which does not exist to exist and that which exists to not exist and so forth. Within this situation, of course, we may be able to perform virtuous actions, but virtue, while it does certainly lead to states of happiness, cannot by itself lead to realization. Only the realization of Mahamudra can lead to liberation. This means that any virtuous action one performs should be embraced by this view or understanding of Mahamudra. If you perform a practice of the creation stage and embrace that practice with Mahamudra, it becomes a cause of liberation; also, if you engage in the slightest action of generosity and embrace that act with the view of Mahamudra, it too becomes a cause of liberation. Any practice of any of the six perfections (paramitas) when embraced by this view, when performed with this view, becomes a cause of liberation. Another way of putting it: any action which is free of conceptualization about the three elements of the action, (the act, the person performing it and the recipient) this Mahamudra view when pervading or embracing all one's actions, can enable one to escape from the jail of samsara and obtain the omniscience of liberation [Buddhahood].

If you rest evenly within this, all of your wrongdoing and obscurations will be burned.

The second line uses the image of fire for Mahamudra. Just as a fire can burn up an entire forest, in this line, Mahamudra is said to be able to burn away all of the wrong-doing and obscurations that one has accrued over a period of time without beginning. In that sense, it is the supreme form of purification. Generally speaking, of course, it is said that if an action that has been performed, (such as a negative action or one of the *ten non-virtuous actions* or one of the *five actions of immediate consequences*) are not confessed or admitted, it will lead to suffering and obstacles and so forth. But the point here is that Mahamudra itself can burn through the imprints or *traces of actions*.[31] As well as one's wrong-doings, the root of wrong-doing itself is obscuration, the obscuration which is mental affliction and the obscuration of the knowable which is ignorance.[32] Obscuration is a powerful obstacle to the practice of meditation and to any practice of virtue. When one's mind is totally overpowered by strong disturbing emotions, one cannot rest in meditation nor engage in active virtue. As well, the obscuration of the knowable, ignorance, is a powerful obstacle. When one is afflicted by a powerful thought of this type of ignorance, fixation and so forth, it obstructs the practice of meditation. But, on the other hand, if one rests in Mahamudra, then this burns through these obscurations. Therefore it says in the third line:

The Benefits of Practicing Mahamudra

This is called for those reasons the torch of the doctrine.

What this means here is that Mahamudra itself, the meaning indicated in the previous lines, is that which illuminates or makes effective all the other aspects of the doctrine. This is not to say that all other practice is unnecessary, otherwise if it were the case that no other practice but Mahamudra were of any value, then the 84,000 different types of teachings given by the Buddha would have been meaningless. In fact, in the practice of Mahamudra we undergo various aspects of training, such as the *four common* and *four uncommon preliminaries*, various forms of *guru-yoga*, yidam practice and so forth. The point here is that these practices are not valueless; the point is that they must be embraced by the view of Mahamudra in order to work. For example, if you perform the prostration practice within the view of Mahamudra, it becomes a very powerful method for the removal of the traces of wrong-doing and the removal of obscurations. This is also true for Vajrasattva practice and so on. Because Mahamudra is therefore that which makes the doctrine, the teachings of the Buddha effective, it is called "the lamp of the doctrine."

Sometimes people who have been practicing for some time can be heard to say that while they have done such and such practices, they have achieved nothing by doing them; they seem to be totally ineffective. The defect in their practice is the absence of the view of Mahamudra. So, if one practices without this understanding, one will not achieve any qualities.

12

The Defects of Not Practicing Mahamudra

The next section deals with the defects of not realizing Mahamudra:

Foolish people who have no interest in this will only be continually carried off by the river of samsara.

What is referred to here is the nature of the mind, which is to be experienced both in meditation and post-meditation. What is being said when it says, "Foolish individuals who have no enthusiasm or interest in this" means that whatever else one does, no matter how virtuous it is – if it is virtuous, it will certainly lead to happiness, comfort and so forth – without the experience of the mind's nature, it will not lead to liberation. Regardless of how pleasant circumstances may become because of temporary acts of virtue, one has not transcended the basic process of samsara and one will be continually carried off by the river of samsara, which means thrown about from one type of existence to the other without any control because the basic root of it has not been cut. The reason why people who are not interested in realizing the nature of the mind are referred to as fools here is because they lack prajna, they lack full or genuine knowledge.

In the sutras, the Prajnaparamita is referred to as "the mother who gives birth to the four types of superiors," which are *shravakas* and *pratyekabuddhas* (the two types of arhats), bodhisattvas and Buddhas. Not only for the realization of a Buddha, but even for the partial realization of the selflessness of an arhat as well as for the twofold realization connected with the Middle-way school of a bodhisattva – the *selflessness of persons* and the *selflessness of phenomena*[33] – this same fundamental prajna, which is the recognition to some extent of the absolute nature of things, must be present. And therefore prajna itself – this one thing – is the deciding factor in liberation. And this is true whether it is Hinayana realization, whether it is Mahayana realization, or whether it is the direct presentation of Mahamudra and the direct identification of the mind's nature as is the case in Mahamudra.

Other acts of virtue that are without the experience of the ultimate nature, while they may lead towards that experience, nevertheless have no decisive immediate benefit because they are of themselves not that recognition, and one is left still spinning in samsara, and spinning one undergoes intolerable suffering. So the line ends with the statement,

Those foolish people experiencing intolerable sufferings in lower states of existence are worthy of compassion.

We have now completed the sixth section which deals with the defects of not practicing Mahamudra. The seventh and final section, which is quite long and detailed, concerns how to practice, the manner of practicing Mahamudra. If you have any questions about what has been presented up to now, please ask.

Questions

Question: "Would you translate the last sentence?"

Translator: One version of the text says "intolerable," another version of the text says "inexhaustible suffering." Then: "Fools [those in lower states of existence] are worthy of compassion."

The Defects of Not Practicing Mahamudra

Question: What are the qualities of what is called "increase"? You were saying that if you don't have the practice of the Mahamudra view, you will not have the qualities.

Rinpoche: Well, it is not said that if Mahamudra is not realized that there will be no qualities, just that there will be no liberation from samsara. So, the qualities that only arise when Mahamudra is realized are the qualities of getting out of the jail of samsara, having all obscurations and imprints of wrong-doing burnt away and possessing the qualities of a Buddha, the thirty-two qualities of maturation which are primarily of the body, and the thirty-two qualities of freedom or abandonment which are primarily of the mind. This involves first of all the total accomplishment of one's own aim, one's own liberation, and the ability through one's wisdom, loving kindness and effectiveness to accomplish the liberation and benefit of others. That's why Mahamudra is referred to here as "the lamp of the doctrine" because it is the lamp which brings all these benefits, all these qualities for the individual who realizes it.

Question: Rinpoche, in Shamatha sometimes I have a thought that comes up and I do not particularly look at it, but boom, it is gone! It disappears so I have not looked at it to examine its parts but it seems to be gone . . .

Rinpoche: That is not really anything at all. Thoughts just do that. Whether you look at them or not, whether you are meditating or not, thoughts vanish. Eventually thoughts just vanish. They do not stay around forever.

Question: In terms of letting go of thoughts it seems as though emotional situations create situations where the thoughts just keep coming up and up again and again.

Rinpoche: Sometimes there is a strong disturbing emotion or strong and persistent thought that arises. When we fail to recognize the root of it, where it starts and comes from, then we get very confused by the branches. The image that is used is that of a tree. In any case, whether you recognize the root of it or not, where this thought, sensation or emotion is coming from, when you meditate, and whatever the thought

95

is, whatever form it takes, looking directly at its nature will cause it to be self-pacified. As far as why this happens: When a tree and its branches start to grow, its branches start to cover the trunk to the extent that in fact you cannot see the trunk; all you can see are the branches of the tree. If the branches falls off or dies, then as that happens you start to see the trunk more and more clearly. In this case, if you look directly at the trunk of a thought, it will vanish or subside.

13

How to Practice Mahamudra

The Manner of Practicing Mahamudra

Of the seven topics of this text, we are now concerned with the seventh, which is how to practice. We have studied the nature of Mahamudra, the realization which has the explained benefits and the absence of realization which has the explained defects. It consists of the view, meditation and conduct discussed above. Nevertheless, simply knowing about these things is of itself of no benefit; it is necessary to put this into practice. In order to put it into practice, one has to understand that practice. If it is properly practiced, then one will generate an extraordinary view and realization; if it is not properly practiced, then one will not.

There are two aspects to what is to be known about how to practice this. The first is how to engage in the preliminaries and the second is how to engage in the main body of the practice.

How to Engage in the Preliminaries

The first section has four aspects.

1. How to Rely Correctly on a Guru and Gain a Correct Ascertainment

Through properly relying on a teacher, one is able to generate stable renunciation. It is through the correct reliance on a teacher and the subsequent generation of stable renunciation that one can enter the door of Mahamudra.

The first thing that one requires in the beginning of one's practice is to properly rely on a teacher. This is discussed in the next two lines of the text:

> *Wishing to attain liberation from intolerable suffering, rely upon a wise guru. When the guru's blessings enter your heart, your mind will be liberated.*

Our situation is that we are in samsara, which is sometimes pleasant and sometimes extremely unpleasant. When it is unpleasant and we are suffering, we cannot tolerate or stand this suffering, either with our bodies or with our minds. When we are happy, at that moment, everything seems okay, except that the happiness never lasts; the circumstances which have produced happiness change, and because of the contrast, the happiness itself becomes a cause of more suffering, which is of the type of suffering called "the suffering of change." Furthermore, the very nature of the situation being instability and constant change is of the nature of suffering, which is called in this case "the pervasive suffering." The basis for practice must therefore be the recognition of this suffering as suffering. And this recognition inspires the genuine desire to be liberated from this.

There are two possible motivations one might have in practicing. One might be the desire for short-term excellence and protection, which refers to the desire to accomplish states of temporary happiness through virtuous actions. While this is a virtuous intention and is connected with virtuous actions, this motivation is not an appropriate motivation for practice as it is not based on a full recognition of the pervasiveness of suffering. The attitude with which one must begin is the attitude of wishing for a final and complete liberation from samsara altogether from having recognized the basic nature of samsara as of the *three sufferings*. This renunciation itself is inspired by correctly relying on a guru.

One might ask why it is necessary to rely upon a guru? The reason why it is necessary to rely upon a guru, in the practice done for the purposes of accomplishing ultimate liberation, is that the situation of such a practice is different from engaging in conventional, mundane activities. When one is attempting to learn or practice something conventionally mundane, then in some situations one will need a teacher, in other situations one will only need one's own intelligence. In either case, one is relying upon intelligence in the conventional sense, either the intelligence of one's teacher and instructor or that of oneself. Here, however, we are concerned with Mahamudra, which in its very nature transcends conceptual mind and therefore is not something that can be figured out through anyone's intelligence. Therefore, the only resource that is available and will enable one to practice Mahamudra is an experienced guru, someone who has experienced it and who has received the transmission of it from a lineage. Experience here means that the guru has to have had an actual experience of dharmata ("the nature of things which transcends the intellect"). And he has to be able to point this out to the student.

Now in the text it refers to the guru as learned or skilled; "rely upon a learned or wise guru." "Learned" here could mean one of two things; it could mean learned in words or learned in their meaning. In this case, a guru who is merely learned in words will not be of much benefit. One needs a teacher who is learned in the meaning, which again means that he has actual experience of the meaning of Mahamudra. An example of the need for this is found in the biography of Naropa, which probably most or all of you have read. Specifically, in the incident where Naropa already had become a great scholar and pandita acting as a professor at Nalanda University. Naropa was sitting outside the temple reading and studying and was approached by a wisdom dakini in the form of an old woman who asked him if he understood the meaning or merely the words. Based upon his response, she predicted that he needed to rely upon Tilopa as a guru who did indeed understand the meaning. The point of this incident is that one always needs to rely upon a teacher who has the experience necessary for him to understand the meaning and not just in the words.

Furthermore, through relying upon such a guru, one becomes engulfed by splendor, which means to say that the guru's blessings enter one's heart and this produces extraordinary experience and realization.[34] So the second aspect of the reason why one has to rely upon such a guru is described in the second line, "When the guru's blessings enter your heart, your own mind will be liberated."

What exactly is the benefit or power of a guru? The true benefit or power of a guru is that one's root guru's power somehow is transferred to you or actually enters into your heart, and the benefit of this is that it causes your heart to be liberated. What this means is that while in general our minds are so bound by concepts of existence and non-existence, fluctuating between the two and so forth, that we will in fact not allow ourselves to become liberated. The process that we usually go through is one of constantly increasing a fixation and resultantly constantly increasing the degrees of disturbing emotions or mental afflictions. If, on the other hand, you generate stable renunciation and devotion for an authentic root guru that goes along with that, then these conditions of renunciation and devotion together with the authenticity of the guru free your mind from or cut through this net of conceptuality and that brings about liberation. So for that reason as well, it is necessary to rely upon a skilled guru.

So, having from the beginning relied upon an authentic guru, the second thing that is necessary is the meditation upon or the cultivation of renunciation, described in the next two lines of the text:

> *These things of samsara are meaningless or pointless, the causes of suffering. And since all of these things that have been done or made are pointless, look at that which is meaningful.*

Our situation of wandering throughout the three realms of samsara is that our minds internally are very childish and easily deceived and distracted, and the external appearances which we perceive seem very impressive and very vivid. Because of the combination of having a childish mind and that childish mind undergoing very impressive and vivid appearances, we become extremely distracted and as a result spend our lives – from the time we are born until the time we die – confused and agitated. The way we think with our mind is based on this confusion. The way we talk, the way we speak and the way we use our speech adds to this confusion, and we engage in a great deal of physical activity or work which is totally involved with this confusion based upon the apparent impressiveness of appearances and the childish attitude of our mind. All of this leads to a situation in which there is no real fruit or no real essence – nothing gained. Furthermore, this can never free us forever from suffering. In fact, although it may appear – when not thoroughly examined – to produce short-term benefit, even this is not true. If one analyses the actual result of one's actions, one sees that not only are they of no benefit to oneself, they actually make one miserable. Our concerns based on our relationship to our experiences or appearances lead us to be in a more or less constant state of worry or anxiety. The type of speech we engage in almost invariably promotes attachment or aversion, which causes us both mental and physical suffering. And the physical activity we engage in is mostly a cause of actual physical pain. Furthermore, the end of any of these circumstances is their destruction – the end of anything that has been constructed is its destruction. The end of anything that has been accumulated is its exhaustion; the end of any form of companionship is separation, and the end of any birth or arising is death. So, things of the world, as said here, are of no use whatsoever. And one should not invest one's intention or energy into these concerns, but rather as the text says, "look at that which is meaningful," which means that nature which is *döndam* ("absolute truth") and Mahamudra, which itself brings fruition, brings liberation when attended to. It is called "the meaningful having an essence of fruit" because this practice of Mahamudra as opposed to conventional, worldly activities produces not only short-term happiness but long-term happiness and final liberation. It produces short-term happiness because the state produced through practice is a tranquil and happy one. But principally, it produces ultimate liberation, which is the omniscience of full Buddhahood and the final end of all suffering.

So the actual cultivation of meditation is definitely necessary. One has to begin by relying upon an authentic guru and be engulfed by that guru's splendor or blessing, then one actually has to meditate and one has to keep on practicing. The situation called "abandoned meditation" (like having acquired some wealth and then been careless with it) is not appropriate. When one has begun to accomplish the practice of meditation, it is necessary to foster, stabilize and make one's experience genuine.

So the first of these four preliminaries is correct reliance upon an authentic guru and the cultivation of renunciation. The second as discussed in the immediately following lines of the text, is the correct ascertainment of the view of meditation and conduct.

In the classification of the topics or subtopics of this text, the first branch of the preliminaries of Mahamudra practice is relying upon a guru and the cultivation of devotion and renunciation. This first branch of what is called "preliminaries" here refers to what we normally call the "preliminaries of *Ngöndro*," and principally the practice of guru-yoga. The function of guru-yoga is explained in "The Lineage Supplication"[35] which says, "Devotion is the head of meditation, as is taught. The guru opens the treasury gate to the treasury of oral instruction. To the meditator who continually supplicates you, grant your blessing that genuine devotion is born within." The first of the preliminaries of Mahamudra, of guru-yoga, includes what we normally think of as "the four common preliminaries," or the four thoughts which turn the mind, and the "four uncommon preliminaries," the four parts of the Ngöndro. From this point of view, all of these practices are branches of guru-yoga.

The next line explains the correct ascertainment of the view in the words,

If you are beyond all grasping at an object [the apprehended] and grasping at a subject [the apprehending], that is the monarch of all views.

"Apprehended" refers to fixation on that which appears as apprehended objects other than oneself and "apprehending" refers to fixation on that which appears as an apprehending cognition. If one's view totally transcends these two types of fixation (fixation upon apparent objects and an apparent subject), then this is called "the king of views." From among the two types of view (the inferential view of the sutras and the experiential view of the tantras), this refers to the experiential view.

The next line describes meditation as follows:

If there is no distraction, it is the monarch among all meditations.

Normally we may regard meditation as an act of thinking, "I am meditating" and trying to bind or press the mind into shape. This, in fact, is not Mahamudra meditation. There must be a fundamental recognition of this nature of Mahamudra, and then one simply rests within that recognition, endeavoring not to be distracted from it. It is not a matter of creating anything or manufacturing or faking anything in the mind; it is a matter of resting in a recognition of this nature, which can be called either "Mahamudra" or "dharmata" and so forth.

The next line explains conduct in the words:

If there is no effort, that is the monarch among all conducts.

What this means is that within the fostering of this recognition of the mind's nature, one's actions are without contrived intention, therefore without contrived action they are spontaneous. Then this mode of action or activity will cause one's experience and realization to flourish, to increase, and this is therefore what is appropriate – the king of actions.

Discussing the result, Tilopa says:

When there is no hope and no fear, that is the final result, and the fruition has been attained or revealed.

What obstructs the accomplishment of the fruition is the hope of some fruition or result attained in the future and the anxiety that it may not happen. If one can transcend this hope and anxiety with regard to some future attainment and experience the presence of fruition within oneself in the present, then it will become actualized or manifest.

Having presented the ascertainment of the view, meditation, conduct and fruition, the text then goes on to explain

2. The Ground, Path, and Fruition

The explanation of the ground is in the line:

It is beyond being an object of conceptual focus, and the mind's nature is lucidity.

The first part of the line means that the mind cannot be said to exist, to not exist, to both exist and not exist, nor to neither exist or not exist; it is beyond any form of conceptual designation. And yet at the same time it is not just nothing; its nature is a manifest clarity or lucidity. And its nature is referred to in the terms of scholars as "the unity or integration of emptiness and clarity."

That being the ground, the next line presents the path in the words:

There is no path to be traversed and yet, in that way you enter the path to Buddhahood.

Generally speaking, we conceptualize the nature of the path thinking, "I am in samsara and I must get from here to there. I must traverse such and such a path," and we use the traditional characterization of the path as the *five paths, ten stages* and so forth, but in fact there is no special path in that sense. The path simply consists of a correct recognition of the ground, and this is one of the implications of the common quotation, "To genuinely view that which is genuine or perfect will bring genuine liberation." The point is that the nature of the ground is in itself perfect or pure and aside from a correct viewing or correct recognition of this ground, there is no other path.

The next line discusses the fruition in the words:

There is no object of meditation, but if you become accustomed to this, you will attain unsurpassable awakening.

What this means is that there is nothing to be meditated upon, and it is in fact facilitation with or getting used to this process of not meditating upon anything that is the meditation which will produce the result. There is a saying attributed to Lord Gampopa that points this out in the words, "As it is certainly meditation, do not attempt to remove the apparent defects of torpor and excitement. If you try to remove these, you will become like a frog trying to jump into the sky."

So, among the four topics connected with the preliminaries in this section of the text, we have completed the first two.

3. How to Abandon Distraction and Rely Upon Isolation

This topic is discussed in the text in the following lines:

Thoroughly examine mundane things or the things of the world. If you do, you will see that none of them persist, none of them are capable of permanence, and in that sense, they are like dreams and magical illusions. Dreams and magical illusions are meaningless. Therefore, generate renunciation and abandon mundane concerns.

The context for this explanation is the common context. The point is that the things of this world are not stable or permanent and in that sense they are like dreams, like what is seen in a dream or like magical illusions. Not only being impermanent, they are also fruitless or meaningless, not established and empty in that sense as well. So, one is advised in these lines to be without craving and attachment for things of the world, to cultivate contentment and to abandon mundane activities.

The next line says:

Cut through the bonds of attachment and aversion toward those around you and your surroundings.

The point of this line is that all connections one has with objects of ordinary perception, of confused perception, are usually of one or the other of two types: One's connection with these is usually either based on attachment or aversion/aggression on one's own part. It is said that in connection with what one experiences with those around one, one's attachment is like boiling water, and one's aversion is like a blazing fire. Attachment occurs whenever one identifies with someone or something as "mine," "my friend, my family, or someone who will help me." Aversion occurs whenever one identifies with someone or something as one's enemy; one thinks, "This is my enemy," which produces aversion and also anger. Most of the connections we make with others and what is around us are of one of these two types, and either type of connection is not beneficial to oneself because any form of attachment (while in its manner it is a desire to be happy) is in its nature worry and fear, agitation and misery. The nature of the states of mind of aversion, aggression, anger and the like is also misery. Not only does this type of attitude and those connections cause oneself to suffer, the actions in which one engages based upon these connections produce suffering for others as well. So, one is advised in these lines to sever all these connections.

The next line gives instruction as to what the alternative is. If one is to sever all connections, what is one to do?

Meditate in isolated retreats, forests, and so forth, living alone.

Having been instructed to remain in solitude, having severed all samsaric connections, the next line tells one what to do while in retreat:

Remain in that state without meditation.

Normally, when we think of meditation in solitary retreat, we assume it involves doing or thinking or meditating upon something, but actually the meditation that is being explained here is simply the transcendence of confused projections through allowing oneself to rest in the experience of the nature of one's mind, and there is no process of practice other than the one set forth in this context. What is recommended here is to cultivate the samadhi of Mahamudra in solitude. And the benefit of practicing in solitary retreat is the clarity and tranquillity of the samadhi that can be developed under those circumstances.

At the same time, it is not the case that it is necessary to cultivate this practice of Mahamudra in retreat only – it is not the case that it can only be done in retreat. The traditional examples of the various styles of practice that Mahamudra can take are exemplified in the biographies of the eighty-four mahasiddhas of India; one can read about each in their biographies and see that each had their own particular lifestyle and their own particular style of practice. For example, Nagarjuna was a great scholar who composed a vast amount of treatises while at the same time ruled over or protected a large set of communities of the ordained *sangha*. While fulfilling his responsibilities as a figure in the sangha and while composing many treatises on previously unknown areas of knowledge, he was still able to practice Mahamudra and obtain supreme siddhi [enlightenment]. Another example is King Indrabhuti who reigned over a considerable region and consequently lived in the midst of great luxury, having a magnificent palace and wonderful retinue and so forth. Yet in the midst of all this luxury, he had no attachment for anything and was able to practice Mahamudra in his specific situation and attain supreme siddhi. Another example is Lord Tilopa himself, whose lifestyle and times were fairly low or poor. At one point he devoted himself to grinding sesame seeds to obtain oil and while in the midst of that work was able to meditate on Mahamudra and obtain supreme siddhi. So regardless of the different lifestyles the siddhas pursued, what they all had in common was that they all in their own particular way fostered this recognition of the mind's fundamental nature and maintained a mental discipline, which means they did not allow their minds to run wild or free.

One can also see a similar diversity of lifestyle in the practitioners who arose in Tibet when the doctrine of Mahamudra spread to that country. Generally speaking, Naropa's student Marpa, his student Milarepa, and his student Gampopa, are referred to as the three forefathers of the Kagyu teachings. These three teachers exemplified three quite different lifestyles. Marpa was quite wealthy and had a family with seven sons and was engaged in a variety of mundane activities necessary in order to maintain that situation, yet at the same time with his practice of Mahamudra he was able to attain supreme siddhi in that lifetime. On a conventional level, one can say that he was quite attached to his family. There was one occasion in India when Naropa prophesied to Marpa, "Your dharma lineage will flourish like the current of a vast river, but your family line will disappear like a sky flower." Marpa responded, "Thank you very much for the first prophecy. Is there anything we can do to change the second? I have seven sons. Surely at least one of these will be able to produce a family lineage." Naropa responded, "Never mind seven sons. Even if you have a thousand, you won't be able to change this." So while on a conventional level he might appear to have been attached to his family, he still was able to practice and accomplish Mahamudra. Marpa's student Milarepa, on the other hand, lived his whole life in circumstances of utmost simplicity, asceticism and freedom from unnecessary activity. Milarepa's student Gampopa exemplified yet a third lifestyle, which is that of an ordained monk who lived within and ruled over an ordained sangha or community. The point of these three examples is that there is no one lifestyle that is itself a sufficient cause for the realization of Mahamudra and there is no one lifestyle that is necessary for the realization of Mahamudra. What is necessary and sufficient is the cultivation of the samadhi of Mahamudra under any circumstances.

How to Practice Mahamudra

If you practice or cultivate the samadhi of Mahamudra, then you will achieve the realization of Mahamudra. This is mentioned in the next line:

When you attain that which is without attainment, you have attained Mahamudra.

The expression "that which is without attainment" means that what is attained when you attain Mahamudra is not something new. All that happens is that the previously unrevealed, unrecognized nature, dharmata, is revealed. Normally we do not recognize this nature and are confused. Through receiving and applying the instructions of one's guru, one becomes free of confusion, and confused projection or experience is replaced by unconfused experience. And this unconfused mode of experience is here referred to as "the attainment that is without attainment."

Then the text goes on:

For example, if the single root of a tree with a trunk and many branches, leaves, flowers and fruit is cut, the ten thousand or one hundred thousand branches will automatically die. In the same way, if the root of mind is cut through, the branches and leaves of samsara will dry up.

The point is that while Mahamudra is essentially one path, one practice, nevertheless through this one path, through this one practice, one accomplishes freedom from all the various types of suffering there are.

There are a variety of different types of suffering in samsara. There are the sufferings of the hell realms (extreme heat and cold), the sufferings of the *preta* realms (hunger and thirst) and so forth; the various sufferings of the *six realms*. As well, there are different causes to these various types of suffering, different disturbing emotions that produce these different circumstances. Now while one may think that in order to remove or free oneself from each result of suffering and each causal disturbing emotion, one needs to apply a specific remedy for each, this is not the case. While it is true that the Buddha did teach 84,000 different types of dharma to serve as remedies for 84,000 different types of disturbing emotions and resultant sufferings, nevertheless in this approach of *männag* ("special instruction"), instead of resorting to different antidotes or remedies, the one remedy is to reveal or recognize this one nature that is the nature of mind and the nature of each and every thing. When this nature is recognized, then through the power of that recognition, all the various disturbing emotions come to be abandoned and as a result all the various types of suffering come to be transcended.

4. The Benefits of Meditation Upon Mahamudra

Describing the result or benefit of meditating on the mind's nature, the text continues:

For example, just as the darkness that has accumulated over a thousand eons is dispelled by the illumination of one lamp or one torch, in the same way, one instant of the wisdom of the clear light of one's mind dispels all of the ignorance, wrongdoing and obscurations accumulated throughout numerous eons.

Imagine a place that has been sealed up in total darkness for a very long time, has received no sunlight, no moonlight, no starlight, no lamplight or any kind of light. When we think about such a place, such darkness, we think of it as though the darkness itself had some substantiality that had to be removed, as though the darkness itself were stable, thick or substantial. And yet, regardless of how long that place has been without any form of illumination (whether one year, a *kalpa* or a thousand kalpas), as soon as a light is lit in that room, light is present and all darkness (regardless of how long it has been there) is dispelled in one instant. In the same way, the nature of the mind of each and every one of us has always been this clear light or luminosity, which is referred to in the *Nyingma* tradition as Samantabhadra and in the *Sarma*[36] tradition as Vajradhara. While this has always been present, it has never been recognized, and this darkness, which is an absence of recognition, has been going on over a period without beginning. Through not recognizing it, we have become confused. And yet through the circumstances and conditions of one's guru's instructions, of one's guru's blessing, of one's own practice and devotion, it is possible for recognition of this nature to occur for the first time. When full recognition of this nature occurs, in that instant all obscuration is dispelled, in the same way as the darkness in the sealed room is dispelled when a lamp is lit.

The realization of Mahamudra is therefore said to be very powerful because if it is complete realization, it removes in one instant three things, which are: "ignorance" *ma-rig-pa*, "wrongdoing" *tig-pa* and "obscuration" *drö-pa*. Ignorance is the opposite of *rig-pa* or "awareness." And the presence of awareness (or the absence of ignorance) is awareness of what is expressed in the Mahayana as dharmadhatu, in the Hinayana as the selflessness of persons and in the Vajrayana as the unity of clarity and emptiness. That awareness (which is the opposite of ignorance) which realizes this is called *rigpa yeshe* or "the wisdom which is awareness." So, any form of failure to recognize this nature is articulated in different sections of the teaching. Whether one talks about the failure to see the nature which is the selflessness of persons, or the absence of recognition of the emptiness of all things, or the absence of recognition which is the nature of Mahamudra, all of this is ignorance or *ma-rig-pa*. Fundamentally, both of the primary types of obscuration (the obscuration of the knowable and the obscuration which is mental afflictions) both stem from ignorance, *ma-rig-pa*. Therefore, awareness (which is the opposite of *ma-rig-pa*, which is the absence of ignorance) is that which realizes all of these things presented in the various sections of the teachings – it realizes the selflessness of persons, it realizes the emptiness of all things, and it realizes Mahamudra.

The second thing dispelled by this realization is wrongdoing, which means the karmic accumulation or imprint of actions. Being under the power of ignorance, our actions or karma produce imprints and negative actions, referred to as "obscurations or veils." All of this (this ignorance and the result of wrongdoing and other forms of obscuration) is beginningless, yet at the same time this one remedy of lucid wisdom that recognizes dharmata ("the nature of all things") can dispel it in an instant, and this is to illustrate the profundity and power of this realization.

Questions

Question: Rinpoche, the text said that the practice of Mahamudra involves no focus or mindfulness of the mind with particular focus. Another teaching from Tilopa's text is that whenever a klesha arises you look directly at it. So, it seems as if in the practice of Mahamudra you are going from an unfocused resting of the mind to a focused direct looking at something, a klesha, or whatever. Particularly this movement from non-focus to focus becomes difficult in post-meditation when there are so many distractions. I experience this when driving down Granville during rush hour. You become fearful, anxious, but you must pay attention to the road, and then to look at the mind undistractedly at this time seems very difficult.

Rinpoche: First of all, in essence, as you say, there is no object of meditation or object of focus in Mahamudra, but that is from the point of view of an unconfused or unbewildered state. From the point of view of a bewildered context, there is a focus. There is an object. For example, you mentioned what you do when a thought arises. When a thought arises, then at the initial moment of directing your awareness to looking at the nature of that thought, there is as you indicated a conceptual focus. Because the thought arising is a bewilderment, it is a relative truth and is bewilderment; so you are entering a context or working in a context of bewilderment. When you see the nature of that thought, through having focused on that thought's nature, when you actually see that nature, the thought is not there; there is no focus. So when you look, there is a focus, but when you see, there is no focus. With regard to post-meditation, in fact, the essence of post-meditation practice is simply not being distracted from whatever you are doing. There is far less danger in driving if you are not distracted, if you are mindful or alert, than there is in driving if you are distracted. So in fact, post-meditation mindfulness and alertness should alleviate the fear of an accident on Granville Street. [laughter]

Question: Rinpoche, if the nature of all things is emptiness, and if we look at the bubble and it pops and there is nothing there, if we look at fear and we touch it and there is nothing there, I'm just wondering about when we look at family or friends. Are they also bubbles, when we touch them and they pop and there is nothing there? Is it the same emptiness?

Rinpoche: There exist of course, logical demonstrations of the emptiness of all things and all persons. But these are not applied or entertained in the context of meditation practice because we are concerned with direct experience, and the easiest direct experience of emptiness is the direct experience of the emptiness or nature of your own mind. So in the practice of Mahamudra, we do not analyze or examine the existential status of external objects or persons, but only of thoughts that can be experienced directly without recourse to analysis. It is said in our tradition, "Do not attempt to get rid of or create or alter external appearances. Just leave them as they are, because they do you no harm and bring you no benefit." The external appearances are not the issue here; it is the mind and the mind's grasping, which is thought. Therefore, we take thought and mind as the basis for meditation.

Question: Rinpoche, I wonder if you could give some clarity on the meditation instruction in Mahamudra. I understand that the meditation when kleshas arise is to feel the texture of that klesha, feel the context of the klesha, feel the essence of the distraction without the content. Is this similar to looking directly at the klesha?

Rinpoche: These two ways of working with kleshas are different; they are distinct. The approach that you described in which you try to feel the texture, as you put it, of the klesha, and appreciate the origin of the klesha and so on, as you explained it, is based upon maintaining the concept or the illusion of the klesha's existing in the first place. Basically what you are doing in such an approach is treating the klesha as something. Here what is being done is not working with what the klesha *seems* to be, but what it really is. In looking directly at it without becoming concerned with the appearance of it – which klesha it is and so on – then you experience it as being more like nothing than being something. The significance of this is that the actual way that you let go of kleshas is through determining their non-existence, through seeing that they have no substantial existence whatsoever. The technique here is to look directly at them and in that way see their nature. What you see or what you experience was explained earlier in the text as seeing them as ripples on water or designs drawn on the surface of water. As they are emerging, they are dissolving already.

Question: Rinpoche, this is a question on mixing. How do you mix the practice of Mahamudra and working as a scholar, especially for us as dharma students, or for myself, as someone who is learning new concepts and accumulating knowledge? How do we mix them together?

Rinpoche: Something that is important to understand about mixing in general, and especially in the context that you just brought up, is what does and what does not constitute distraction. It was said by Tilopa, "Child, it is not by appearances that you are fettered, but by craving. Therefore Naropa, relinquish or cut through craving." The distinction needs to be made between appearances and our craving for or grasping at them. Appearances themselves are not a problem. Grasping or craving is problematic. When you study you are training your intellect through the acquisition of knowledge and training yourself in learning more efficiently and so forth. That training of the intellect, that cultivation of the prajna of study is not a problem, because essentially what you are working with is the cognitive lucidity, which is one of the qualities of your mind, the other quality being emptiness. The problem is grasping at the concepts or fixating on the concepts acquired through study or knowledge. The way to work with this is simply to study in a way in which you cultivate a mindfulness within the performance of study analogous to that of meditation, and if there is mindfulness while you are studying, and alertness, then the study will not generate grasping and in that way can be mixed to some extent with practice.

Question: One should not have a fixation upon achieving any particular end in Mahamudra. But when the Buddha sat under the bodhi-tree, he said definitely that he is not getting up until he has achieved an end.

Rinpoche: Generally speaking, any aspect of the view, meditation and conduct studied by any type of Buddhist in any form of Buddhist approach has two aspects to it. Any level of the teaching is concerned with both relative truth, how things appear, and with absolute truth, how things really are. In this context, what we are concerned with – and this is true for any level of the teaching (it is true for the shravaka approach of view, meditation and conduct, it is true for the bodhisattva approach within the Mahayana and it is true for both the Mahamudra and Dzogchen approaches within the Vajrayana) – when we say, "Have no hope or anxiety for a result" is about how to actually foster the mind's nature, and therefore this is an explanation on how to experience absolute truth and is not concerned with the progression of relative truth. This is not unique to Vajrayana. Even in the context of the shravaka path, where the view is the selflessness of persons, from the point of view and on the level of absolute truth in that vehicle, since there is no personal self, there is nothing to be abandoned, nothing to be realized and so forth. This is also true in the Mahayana: from the point of view of the Middle-way, there is nothing to be abandoned, nothing to be realized and so forth. And of course this is true, as we have seen, in Mahamudra. But such an explanation is from the point of view of the mind's nature, from the view of absolute truth. In the context of viewing conventional or relative truth, then each one of these approaches or paths would have its own fruition. In the case of the shravaka path, there is the attainment of *arhatship*; in the case of the Mahayana, there is the attainment of the *bodhisattva levels* and Buddhahood; in the case of the Mahamudra, there is the attainment of supreme siddhi and Buddhahood.

So, in fact, it was said by the Buddha when he first sat under the bodhi-tree at Bodhgaya, "My body may dry up, my bones and flesh may rot, but I shall not move from this seat until I achieve the very essence of awakening."

Question: "What is the difference between being empty and being spaced-out?"

Rinpoche: Well, there is a great difference. States of being spaced-out, such as a state of *Shamatha* that is totally devoid of clarity for example, are characterized by this absence of clarity, which is an absence of prajna, an absence of intelligence. Being spaced-out is essentially a state of stupidity. And it is characterized by being without thought, being without conceptuality. But that absence of conceptuality is really a sort of a stupid acuity. This is something that is similar in some ways to the state of the formless realms, such as the formless realm perception of there being nothing and yet there not being nothing. Whereas, a recognition of the fundamental nature, dharmata the nature of the mind or whatever you want to call it is wisdom that has the characteristic of absolute certainty and of being unshakeable in its certainty. It has been said about this by siddhas in the past that when you have this recognition, that even if 100 Buddhas appeared in the sky in front of you and said, "That's not it," you would say, "Yes, it is" because you have seen it directly. For example, I can see the vajra that is on the table in front of me, and having seen it, even if 100 people were to say to me, "There is no vajra on that table in front of you," I would think of their argumentation as meaningless. It would not shake my conviction that there is a vajra there because I have actually seen it. So, it's a state of wisdom that is totally without doubt.

14

The Main Practice of Mahamudra

How to Engage in the Main Body of Practice

This section is the main practice and is divided into four sections, the first being

1. The Practice for Those of Highest Faculties

The explanation of the practice from the point of view of those of the highest faculties begins with Tilopa's expression of delight in Mahamudra itself:

Kye ho

This delight encompasses delight in two aspects. The first is appropriateness in experiencing delight in Mahamudra in that one accomplishes one's own benefit. Through the practice of Mahamudra, one need not go through three periods of innumerable kalpas of gathering accumulations in order to accomplish awakening but rather one can through this practice accomplish the state of unity, the state of Vajradhara, in one body, in one lifetime. It is in that way easy and, not only easy, it is also extraordinarily powerful, as was explained in the previous verse which showed how Mahamudra dispels all the obscurations of ignorance and so forth that there are. So when Tilopa says "Kye ho" in expressing his delight in this, he is also expressing his delight in the possibility of actually communicating or transmitting Mahamudra to someone else, in this case to Naropa. This is in contrast to the Buddha's exclamation soon after his awakening, when he said, "I have found a profound, tranquil dharma that transcends all elaborations and is like healing nectar, yet no matter to whom I would explain this, no one would be able to understand it. Better I remain silent." This expression of sadness on the Buddha's part is understood as being a way of expressing the profundity of dharma. In any case, in this instance Tilopa is not expressing himself in that way but is sharing his genuine delight in the fact that there is someone to whom Mahamudra can actually be transmitted and therefore someone else whom it can directly benefit.

The next line says:

The intellect cannot see that which is beyond conceptual mind.

The nature of the conceptual mind or intellect is that it cannot see or experience that which is not conceptual in nature; it cannot see what is beyond it.

The next line says:

You will never realize that which is uncreated through created dharmas.

This means that any attempt to fabricate realization – through the use of inferential reasoning which tries to figure out or ascertain the nature of the mind through the use of fabricated meditations – cannot do any more than create; it cannot truly bring one to discover the fundamental nature.

In this way, through the presence of conceptualization or conceptual fabrication we fail to realize this nature of the mind. Therefore different forms of deviations or mistakes that can occur through the presence of the tendency to intellectualize are pointed out in the Kagyu traditional meditation instructions. These are traditionally explained as mistakes one makes with regard to emptiness and are called "turning emptiness into an antidote or remedy, turning it into a seal," literally "getting lost in its being the ground of all that is to be known, all that is knowable." When it says "getting lost into emptiness as a seal," it means for example that when a disturbing emotion arises we would generate the attitude, "Oh, this is no problem because its nature is empty," but that is just an intellectual attitude; it's not an experience. Seal in this case means trying to seal your experience with an intellectual or conceptual notion of emptiness. With regard to "getting lost into emptiness of the ground of all that is knowable," what it means is again trying to conceptually generate a certainty or an experience that emptiness is the nature of all things. While from one point of view such certainty or ascertainment is good, nevertheless because it is just a concept, it is not appropriate in the practice of Mahamudra and is therefore a deviation. Then, deviation with regard to "getting lost into emptiness as an antidote" is the attitude, for example, that if you conceptually meditate on emptiness, the disturbing emotion will disappear when it arises. What all these three types of errors have in common is that they are all conceptual and are an attempt to produce something through the application of concepts.

Now the alternative to these, that which is unmistaken, is not a deviation, it is the direct experience of dharmata or "the nature of things" which transcends concept, transcends intellect and which is not fabricated, not produced or constructed by any kind of intellect or concept. The text explains this in the lines:

If you wish to attain or realize that which is beyond the intellect and is uncreated, then scrutinize your mind and strip awareness naked.

The word translated as "scrutinize" literally means "to cut the root." It is like if something has been stolen and you are looking for it, so it means an intended search for something. The point of this is that to actually experience this nature there has to be a direct, non-conceptual experience of it, and one's attention or energy is put into that, not into attempting to conceptually generate the experience.

There are two possible ways to understand the scrutiny of mind. One might consider scrutiny of mind to be watching the mind and thinking, "Now I am thinking. Now I am happy. Now I am sad. Such and such a disturbing emotion is arising in me" and so forth. Other than during a certain point in the practice of Shamatha this has no benefit and is not what is meant by the scrutiny of mind here. Here what is meant is looking directly at the mind without saying that it is one thing or another, to experience its nature just as it is, this nature of the mind that can be seen as empty, lucid or as both. And it is this that we have not yet recognized. What must be done to recognize this is that one must rest in what is called "naked or unveiled awareness." The term "naked" here means direct, with nothing in-between, no concept or any other kind of veil in-between that which is looking for the mind and that mind which is being looked for, so, totally direct, with nothing in-between. Normally we do not look at things that way; normally we process everything we experience through a veil or a border of intellectualization. As long as we do that, as long as we do not abandon that, we will never experience the direct nature with nothing in-between.

There are many different approaches to the guidance or instructions in meditation. As Patrul Rinpoche said, "Some are better than others." Generally speaking, there are two approaches, one is called "the guidance through words of a pandita" and the other is called "guidance through experience of a meditator." The guidance through words of a pandita tends to be elaborate, with a lot of references to other texts and a complete philosophical underpinning to what is presented. While this type of text and approach is elegant, it is not profound in the sense that it is not practical in application. The experiential guidance of a meditator is less elegant as literature and certainly less complicated, but it is practical in the sense that it is easy to understand and therefore easy to use. So, we are advised in this context to abandon the first, guidance through words of a pandita, and make use of the second type of instruction, experiential guidance of a meditator. Obviously, the text we are studying here is of the second variety – this need not be said – because such expressions as "scrutiny of mind," "resting in naked awareness" and so forth are characteristics of this second type of instruction or approach.

The main emphasis in this section of the text and the main emphasis in the presentation of such instructions as "scrutiny of the mind" and "resting in naked, direct awareness" is to let go of intellectual contrivance such as inferential reasoning. Yet, at the same time, having let go of intellectualization per se it is possible to deviate in a further way, namely into attachment to experience. While we say that we are concerned with experiential guidance, then there is a type of experience that can arise that can be deceptive, deceptive in a sense that this experience itself can also veil naked awareness, can prevent one from contacting naked awareness or experiencing naked awareness directly.

There are three different experiences that can arise which can veil awareness in that way. The first is an experience of bliss; a traditional term for this is "being stuck to the glue of the disturbing emotions." This is an experience in meditation where, because of the process of practice, there is some comfort, bliss and joy, and being delighted in this, one identifies with it. But this bliss is not *rig-pa*, it is not "awareness." A similar thing that can happen is an experience of intense lucidity or clarity. One identifies with it and insists, "I see this." There is an experience of some kind of lucid insight and that can also obscure the direct experience of awareness. There can also be an obscuration through the experience of non-conceptuality. All of these are experiences that are distinct from realization. While the nature that is realized when one has actual realization cannot be said not to be blissful and certainly not to be not lucid, nevertheless the quality of this is very different from the quality of mere experience. Mere experience is something the siddhas of the past have said does not last; it is here today and gone tomorrow. Getting caught up in experience does veil one's awareness.

Allow the cloudy water of thought to clarify itself or to clear itself.
Do not attempt to stop or create appearances. Leave them as they are.

What this is dealing with is the fact, as has already been explained, that what we are concerned with is the actual even-placement aspect of actually resting in the state of Mahamudra. This is something we can do as ordinary individuals. By having gone through the process of scrutinizing the mind, looking for the mind in a very precise manner, we thereby come to be able to rest in naked awareness. Nevertheless, from time to time, when one is engaged in the even-placement of Mahamudra, thoughts may arise, and thoughts arise as concepts. Now the nature of thought is conceptual and the nature of the even-placement of Mahamudra is non-conceptual – it transcends the conceptual mind. From that point of view, thoughts could be regarded as something of a problem or defect. However, the way they are regarded is that they are like silt which pervades a body of water that has been stirred-up. Just as one can allow the water to be clarified by allowing it to remain still and the silt will then settle to the bottom, in a similar way, if you allow your mind to rest without being agitated or moved, then the silt of thought will settle down naturally. In that sense, because you don't have to do anything to get rid of thought, thoughts are not regarded as harmful.

As well, in the context of one's relationship to external appearances (things you hear, see, smell and so forth), these are not regarded as a problem either. As Tilopa said to Naropa, "Child, it is not by appearances that you are fettered, but by clinging. Therefore abandon clinging, Naropa." The point of that is the same point that is expressed in this line of the text. You don't have to do anything to appearances themselves or the manner of experience, because appearances themselves are just as reflections in a mirror – they do no harm. So, you don't have to try and stop appearances, i.e. reduce the vividness of appearances, nor do you have to try and abandon them or turn them into anything other than what they are – just let them be as they are and that is sufficient.

The next line of the text says:

If you are without acceptance and rejection of external appearances, all that appears and exists will be liberated as mudra.

The Main Practice of Mahamudra

Any form of Buddhist practice or teaching is included within this threefold presentation, called "the three yanas (Hinayana, Mahayana and Vajrayana)," the lesser, greater and vajra vehicles.[37] All of these are the same in the sense that all were taught in order to be of benefit to beings and in order to tame or subdue the disturbing emotions of those for whom those particular vehicles are appropriate. So all of them are of the nature of the path. The distinction that can be made between them is that there are three different methods or approaches to dealing with the disturbing emotions, so they are distinct in their remedy and in their approach to the development of qualities. In the Hinayana or lesser vehicle, the approach is to abandon or relinquish the disturbing emotions. The disturbing emotions are identified as bad or problematic, and through cultivating an intense desire to be free of them, one manages to abandon them.

The approach taken in the second vehicle, the greater Mahayana vehicle, is one of transformation. While the disturbing emotions continue to arise naturally, by embracing them with *bodhichitta*, they are slowly and gradually transformed. For example, one's tendency to divide the world into friends and enemies and to have attachment to the former and aversion towards the later is gradually transformed by the development of one's loving kindness and compassion into an all-pervasive bodhichitta that embraces all beings.

The third Vajrayana vehicle takes another approach in that it takes the disturbing emotions as the path. What taking the disturbing emotions as the path or bringing them to the path means, for example in the case of the disturbing emotion of aversion, through looking at it directly, one discovers that in its nature it has no true existence and is therefore not a solid thing as it might have appeared to be, and through recognizing the fundamental nature of the disturbing emotion brings it to the path, so to speak. What this means in this context is that one must not develop the attitude, "I must abandon this, I am going to abandon this." But one also does not accept or cultivate or get involved with the disturbing emotions the way an untrained person would. What this means is that one neither views the disturbing emotions as one's enemies nor allows oneself to become attached to and involved with them.

The text continues:

The all-basis is unborn, and without that unborn all-basis, abandon or relinquish habits, wrongdoing, and obscurations.

What it means when it says "the all-basis is unborn" can refer both to the primordial all-basis and to the present all-basis,[38] which is the basis for that which contains the imprints of habits. In any case, through the fact that this is unborn, there is no solidity for habits to rest in, i.e. if this nature is directly perceived, then one does not have to intentionally abandon these obscurations because they are seen through, their nature and the nature of that which they obscure is seen directly and they do not have to be separately abandoned.

Then the text continues

Therefore, do not fixate or reckon. Rest in the essence of the unborn or in the unborn nature.

This means that if you perceive this nature directly, then you don't have to worry, figure out or reckon whether or not you will be able to abandon the disturbing emotions; you do not have to engage in the process of thinking, "Well, I can abandon this disturbing emotion and don't seem to be able to abandon that disturbing emotion. I probably will be able to abandon this disturbing emotion" and so on, because you are working much more directly by seeing the nature, what is behind, beneath or in the midst of all this. So it is inappropriate or unnecessary to worry about the abandonment of the disturbing emotions. From this point of view, when they arise, it is fine; when they don't arise, it also fine because the nature itself (which is being experienced directly, the dharmata) is unchanging and unaffected by the presence or absence of disturbing emotions. So rather than putting your attention into manipulating disturbing emotions, you are advised to put your attention into just resting within that unborn and unchanging nature.

The next line says:

In that state, appearances are fully apparent; but within that experience of vivid appearances allow concepts to be exhausted or to dissolve.

What this line means is that, again, let appearance, i.e. what is experienced (which is your self-appearance or personal experience), just be; don't attempt to manipulate what you hear, see and so forth, but allow thoughts or fixation, which only solidify that experience, to be exhausted – let go of that.

2. A Restatement of the View, Meditation, Conduct and Fruition from a Resultant Point of View

Following this comes a restatement of the view, meditation, conduct and fruition. Previously we had a four-lined explanation of these, which said, "If you are beyond all grasping at an object and grasping at a subject, that is the monarch of all views. If there is no distraction, that is the monarch among all meditations. If there is no effort, that is the monarch among all conducts. When there is no hope and no fear, that is the final result, and the fruition has been accomplished or revealed." Here it is slightly different. It says:

Complete liberation from all conceptual extremes is the supreme monarch of views. Boundless vastness is the supreme monarch of meditations. Being directionless and utterly impartial is the supreme monarch of conduct. Self-liberation beyond expectation or hope is the supreme result or fruition.

The reason why these four topics are presented in a similar but distinct way twice in the text is that previously what was explained was how to enter into the view, the meditation, the conduct and so forth, how to approach them. Here what is being explained is how they are when one has become trained in or facilitated in them, so more from a resultant point of view.

The point of the first line concerning the view, that "Complete liberation from all conceptual extremes is the supreme monarch of views," is that the supreme view is a view that is without fixation on things as existing or fixation on things as non-existing. Then when it says, "Boundless vastness is the supreme monarch of meditations," boundless here refers to the same quality in one's meditation, cultivating the view that is beyond extremes and experiencing meditation that way and the resultant experience of vastness, total freedom, lack of being hemmed-in in any way. The next line, "Being directionless and utterly impartial is the supreme monarch of conduct," again refers to this same idea in one's conduct being totally beyond reification of existence and non-existence. The result is defined here as being the discovery of that which is abiding within oneself and which is distinct from hoping for a result in the future. These are an explanation of the view, meditation, conduct and result from the point of view of a practitioner of the highest faculties.

The section we have just gone through explaining the actual practice of Mahamudra from the point of view for one of the highest faculties is an explanation that applies to the practice of the sort of person who is said to have simultaneous realization and liberation. Such a person who is of the highest faculties does not really pass through different stages of practice or different stages of experience. The other two types of practitioners, those of average or inferior faculties, are similar in the sense that they have to pass through a certain number of stages of practice or experience in order to come to this realization. And it is this process that is dealt with in the next few lines.

3. The Practice for Those of Medium or Lesser Faculties

For a beginner it is like a fast current running through a narrow bed or a narrow defile.

The Main Practice of Mahamudra

What this means is that when one first starts to cultivate samadhi ("meditative absorption"), there is in general a fluctuation or oscillation between sometimes recognizing the mind's nature and sometimes not being able to do so, sometimes being able to let the mind rest naturally and sometimes not being able to do so. This experience occurs in both contexts of Shamatha [tranquillity meditation] and *Vipashyana* [insight meditation].[39] In either case, there is neither a great deal of stability nor a great deal of continuous clarity or lucidity.

The next line describes what is experienced afterwards:

In the middle or after that, it becomes like the gentle current of the River Ganges.

This is what is experienced when you have become used to the cultivation of samadhi, and at this point (while the mind is not still) there are not many waves, there is not much turbulence, and the speed of mind has slowed down to the point where there is a growing experience of stability and a growing experience of clarity, nevertheless it is not still.

The next line says

In the end, it is like the flowing of all rivers into the mother ocean, or it is like the meeting of the mother and child of all the rivers.

Rather than there being a strong current, even a strong and slow current, there is just a little meandering of the water. This means that while the mind is not absolutely still, there is a great stability and great lucidity to it. In order to accomplish this, most practitioners have to go through the process of experiencing the other stages, working through them by practicing meditation again and again and again.

The next section of the text deals with the actual practice of Mahamudra and is concerned with what methods might be necessary in order for someone with ordinary faculties to pass through these various stages leading to realization. The next line begins this discussion:

Those of little intelligence, if they find they cannot remain in that state, may apply or hold the technique of the breathing and emphasize the essence of awareness.

The term "little intelligence" here means that most people are inferior to someone of the highest capabilities who does not need any other methods or techniques, so it is in comparison with those discussed in the first section. The nature of our being of average faculties is that simply when we start to practice samadhi, sometimes it is clear and sometimes it is not, sometimes it is stable and sometimes it is not. And we have to go through the process of gradually increasing the lucidity and stability of our meditation. When it says, "May apply or hold the technique of the breathing," it refers to instructions traditional among the siddhas of our lineage that one can cultivate samadhi through the application of the middle-breathing, the vase-breathing or the threefold gentle breathe. Concerning the statement, "emphasize the essence awareness," means to tighten awareness. It is true that if someone's awareness is too tightly adjusted they may need to loosen it. Generally speaking, this is not our problem, rather we have too little lucidity and too little stability in samadhi and need to therefore somewhat exert energy in awareness so that we have enough attention to notice what is happening in meditation and to correct defects. So, what is necessary is to engage in methods or techniques which will allow one's mindfulness, attention or attentiveness to become stable.

The text continues:

Through many techniques or branches such as gaze and holding the mind, tighten awareness until it stays put, exerting tension or effort until awareness comes to rest in that state or in its nature.

"Gazes" here refers to the application of the gazes as remedies to the two major defects of meditation, torpor and excitement. It is traditionally taught that if one is afflicted by torpor in meditation, one should raise one's gaze and look up, and if one is afflicted by excitement in meditation, one should lower one's gaze and look down. In any case, one applies these various techniques or remedies to the conscious exertion of awareness or attention until one's awareness abides naturally in the state of clarity. That was the application of techniques or remedies appropriate for someone of average or middle faculties.

In the words of the text, the next line says:

If you rely upon karmamudra, the wisdom of bliss and emptiness will arise.

Generally speaking, karmamudra practice refers to taking desire as the path. And while this can be helpful for one or two very extraordinary individuals in each generation, most people who have attempted to do this have merely increased their disturbing emotions. While it is taught for exactly the opposite reason and purpose, nevertheless this seems to be what happens. So practically speaking, we tend to, in the place of karmamudra, practice the samayamudra or *tummo*.

The practice of tummo is making the utmost use of the channels, winds (*prana*) and drops (*bindu*) of the vajra-body such that one actually generates the wisdom of bliss and emptiness. The way this happens is that through the application of the correct use of the channels, winds and drops, warmth or heat and bliss are generated physically and, with this as a condition, the wisdom of bliss and emptiness is caused to arise in the mind of the practitioner. Referring to this, the text says:

Enter into the union having consecrated the upaya or method and the prajna or knowledge. Slowly let it fall or send it down, coil it, turn it back, and lead it to its proper place.

Then the text goes on to describe part of what this practice consists of through the application and visualization of the fire of tummo, then the drops at the top of the head are caused to slowly descend to circulate, then they are brought back up and dispersed or spread throughout the body so that they pervade the whole body.

The text continues:

Finally spread it or cause it to pervade your whole body. If there is no attachment or craving, the wisdom of bliss and emptiness will appear.

This is the approach which has been used by most practitioners of the Kagyu tradition. In conjunction with the profound method of the "Six Yogas of Naropa," this practice and approach has been known to produce extraordinary realization and extraordinary wisdom.

4. The Result of the Practice of Mahamudra

The next section of the text describes the result of the practice of Mahamudra and says:

You will possess longevity without white hair and you will be as healthy as the waxing moon. Your complexion will be lustrous and you will be as powerful as a lion. You will quickly attain the common siddhis or attainments, and you will come to alight in or attain the supreme siddhi as well.

There are generally speaking two results to the practice of Mahamudra. The first in importance is what is called "the uncommon or supreme siddhi or attainment" and the second is what is called "the common or ordinary attainment." The supreme attainment, the ultimate result, is that through the samadhi of Mahamudra all there is to be abandoned (the disturbing emotions and so forth) are pacified of themselves. Through the self-pacification of all that is to be abandoned, the twofold wisdom of a Buddha – that wisdom which knows what there is and that wisdom which knows exactly how things really are – manifest. That is the supreme siddhi or ultimate result.

With regard to how the common attainments result from the practice of Mahamudra, it says in "The Refuge Ordination Ceremony": "I go for refuge to the dharma, supreme peace and supreme passionlessness." What this means is that through the cultivation of Mahamudra, the pacification of all disturbing emotions, which leads as well to supreme siddhi, in the short run also produces a certain state of mind; it produces a state of mind which is supremely peaceful and placid. Normally our minds are anything but peaceful; we are afflicted by our thoughts, afflicted in a sense that while some thoughts are pleasant, most are unpleasant and are of the nature of agitation and worry. This agitation and worry actually gets to the point where it makes us physically uncomfortable and finally physically sick through its negative influence on the channels and winds. This agitation and worry makes us age more quickly and makes us become ill more easily. The samadhi of Mahamudra produces a state of mental peace and therefore mental bliss and comfort, therefore a state of physical comfort and health, which will cause one to have a long life, without white hair and as the text says, "Your complexion will be lustrous and you will be as powerful as a lion." In any case, the results of Mahamudra are these two, the common or ordinary siddhi in the short run and the ultimate or uncommon siddhi in the long run.

Dedication and Aspiration

Next in the text come the dedication and aspiration, which consist of two lines:

> *These instructions of the essential point of Mahamudra, may they abide in the hearts of worthy or fortunate beings.*

This contains two aspirations, that beings be worthy, i.e. that all beings be able to practice this, and the second that being able to practice this, they have access to it, and receive and keep these instructions in their hearts.

The Colophon

Following, the text concludes with the record of composition and the translation:

> *This was bestowed on the banks of the River Ganges by the great and Glorious Siddha Tilopa, who had realized Mahamudra, upon the Kashmiri pandit who was both learned and realized, Naropa, after Naropa had engaged in twelve hardships or austerities. This was translated and written down at Pullahari in the north by the great Naropa and the great Tibetan translator, the king among translators, Marpa Chokyi Lodro.*

There are different editions of this text which are mostly noticeable by the fact that the text itself will be arranged in a different order. Principally, there are the editions found in *The Collected Works of Lord Pema Karpo* and then the edition I have used which is based on *The Topical Analysis* of Lord Rangjung Dorje, the Third Karmapa.

Questions

Question: Rinpoche, it would seem that having confidence in one's experience would be very important, and at the same time generally confidence is like what you described. I wondered if you could speak about this, and also are there ways that one has to nurture and stabilize confidence?

Rinpoche: Well, experience in this sense refers to different kinds of appearances, not particularly forms but the different kinds of experienced appearance, such as the appearance of bliss, the appearance of lucidity and so forth. The direct experience of naked awareness is entirely different, especially in the sense that it is stable; one can't get rid of it; it won't disappear. When there is a recognition, it will not vanish. Whereas these experiences, as vivid as they may be today, are gone tomorrow. And the best way to relate to them is simply not to be attached to the presence or absence of any kind of experience but simply to keep on, to continue one's practice. So the essence of the approach is to have no attachment for what occurs.

Question: One of Jamgon Kongtrul Lodrö Thaye's songs explained Mahamudra as simplicity, one-taste, and non-meditation. Is that the same as the non-meditation referred to here?

Rinpoche: No. In the section of the *Song of Lodro Thaye* to which you are referring, he is discussing the stages of the practice of Mahamudra meditation. There are generally speaking four stages of Mahamudra experience and realization that are traditionally enumerated: One-pointedness, beyond elaboration (simplicity), one-taste and non-meditation, and these are the stages of the path. Non-meditation in that context refers to a certain level of Mahamudra experience or realization. The instruction here, not to intellectualize and so forth, is something that is to be applied from the very beginning and is therefore not equivalent to the non-meditation as a stage of Mahamudra. We are very obscured by our intellect; we are not obscured by anything else. Our biggest problem in the practice of Mahamudra is that we want things to go well, we want meditation to be very elegant and know exactly what we want it to be. In trying to program our meditation in that way, then we create the circumstances for our own disappointment and come to think, "Oh, it is not going well." Those dynamics are among what is to be renounced, and what is intended by the instruction to simply rest in direct and naked awareness.

Question: It seems to me, of course that this state of meditation is the ground of Mahamudra and we have the path to go on. Is it quite reasonable that we can also remember what the path is when we are practicing? For example, when I receive the teachings on the essence of non-meditation, I can only receive it in a conceptual way and not have the direct experience. Of course, we can transform it, but what I am asking is that it seems to me that the explanations are quite meaningful now in the ultimate sense.

Rinpoche: This can be used right now; all of this can be applied right now. From the point of view of the lower *yanas*, of course there is a long sequential arrangement of practice and the path is seen as very long. But in the uncommon approach of Mahamudra, the path consists of looking at one's own mind. And there should be no great difficulty in looking at your own mind because it is your own mind. This means it is not at all pretending that something that is not empty is empty, that something that does not appear to be empty is empty, that something that does not appear to be lucid is lucid. It has nothing to do with programming or convincing yourself of anything. Of course, it is true that as beginners we have obscurations that we have to deal with, yet these can definitely be dispelled by one's faith and diligence, and there is no real difficulty in this. Whether you consider it the blessing of the Kagyu gurus or your own faith and devotion, in any case if you have trust in the validity of this process, it will definitely occur.

Question: Rinpoche, I wonder if you would talk a little more about shamatha-Mahamudra? It sounds like the enemy of dullness happens without us knowing it is already there. I know that clarity is present, but I am not sure if I know what the distinction is. If someone is sitting and the perception was vivid and there wasn't much thought, is that an indication of clarity or dullness present?

Rinpoche: To the aspect of clarity, which is present in Mahamudra meditation and the absence of the defect of torpor, is the unimpeded experience of appearances, but it is also the certainty of a direct recognition of the mind's nature. Now, certainty here does not refer to inferential certainty; it refers to the certainty that there is a distinct and clear experience of the mind's nature. In general, what is said to be most necessary for the practice of Mahamudra – for example, in *The Moonbeams of Mahamudra* of Takpo Tashi Namgyal – is the two faculties of mindfulness and attentiveness. It is said in *Moonbeams* that there should be as much of these as is possible; the more mindfulness, the more attentiveness, the better. And one should never be apart from these in one's meditation practice for as much as an instant. In fact, mindfulness and attentiveness have to be so clear that they are hard, that there is almost a hard edge to their lucidity. Without that crisp clarity, it will become vague and dark.

Question: You said that we should embrace the view of Mahamudra in every action. My question is what about the boundaries and rules given by society? Do I get rid of them?

Rinpoche: There is absolutely no reason why embracing all actions with the view of Mahamudra should cause them to be in conflict with the customs of the world. In fact, one should act in accordance with the customs of society.

Question: "How?"

Rinpoche: Well, there are three aspects to conduct; there is what you do with your body, what you do with your speech and what you do with your mind. What you do with body and speech is simply to behave properly, which means in accordance with the way of things or the way of the world. In this context, in accordance with the way of the world means to be harmonious with others, not to be in conflict with others, not to be constantly fighting with others. With speech it means not to be impulsive but to speak carefully and with consideration for the effect of one's speech. Now, sometimes we can't do this and we act improperly. The reason we act improperly with body and speech is that our minds are under the control of disturbing emotions. If your mind is not under the control of disturbing emotions, if your mind is in a state of relaxation and tranquillity, then improper actions of body and speech will more likely not occur. So the mind part of conduct is to always experience the nature of the mind. And if you experience the nature of the mind, you will not be overpowered by attachment, aversion and stupidity.

In the beginning, of course, this is difficult. So one can cultivate the attitude from the start, "I own my mind. My mind doesn't own me and run my life. I am going to control and train the mind." The attitude and practice that ensues from this will bring about the pacification of the mind, which will cause the actions of one's body and speech to be in accordance with the needs of everyone.

Question: Rinpoche explained that intellectual mind is a direct obstacle to the realization of the true nature of one's own mind. Does this mean that if I study Buddhist knowledge, I increase the obstacles?

Rinpoche: No. There are two situations with regard to the use of conceptual thought in the dharmic sense. When I said that the conceptual or intellectual attitude could be an obstacle, I was referring to one of them and not to the other. Generally speaking, to study dharma and various areas of knowledge a great deal is not only not an obstacle to the practice and realization of Mahamudra, but it also is a great assistance. What is an obstacle is if you think about it while meditating. This becomes an obstacle that you might make the mistake of thinking that you can figure it out, that you can reason it out by using logic and inferential reasoning. And Mahamudra is not an object of inference; it is not a practice involving trying to reason and figure it out. Mahamudra is allowing direct experience of this nature to occur. So, aside from that particular mistake or mistaken use of study, studying itself should and certainly can stabilize and enhance the practice of Mahamudra and definitely will not hurt it.

Question: I have a lot of difficulty with understanding how to look at the nature of mind. When there is instruction in the text on looking at external appearances without altering them, without projection, is that the same technique that one uses when one looks at one's mind, and if not, what are the actual mechanics of how to look at the nature of your mind?

Rinpoche: These two techniques are slightly different. The difference between looking directly at appearances and looking directly at the nature of the mind is that, because we have a beginningless habit of samsara, we experience external appearances as substantial, and we will continue to experience them as though they had substantial existence until there is some extraordinary level of realization. It is very difficult to work with external appearances in meditation in the beginning, because they seem so solid, and therefore it is recommended in this tradition to just leave them alone, since they are not the problem. They do not particularly pose much harm or help. Your mind, on the other hand, is manifestly insubstantial, and you can experience this by looking for substantiality within it. If you find it difficult to look directly at the mind and perceive its insubstantiality, then you can select various substantial characteristics and look for them in turn. For example, you can look for a color, look for a location, look for a shape, look for a size, and so on. If you take it step by step like that, sooner or later you will definitely come to experience directly the mind's insubstantial nature.

Question: Rinpoche, I have two questions, if I may. The first is about kindness and how kindness seems to arise from space. Through your great blessings and not my merit particularly, I have some experience and understanding of resting in clarity. I am wondering how it is that when one really does rest the mind and allow that experience of the insubstantiality, the vastness [to arise], that from that arises a feeling of rawness and tenderness and a longing to be more kind to others?

Rinpoche: This sounds good. In the Third Karmapa's *Aspirational Prayer of Mahamudra* he says that beings in their nature are always Buddha, but through not realizing this they wander in samsara. This type of understanding is something that you naturally arrive at through experiencing your mind's nature. When you experience to some extent your mind's nature, then right away you experience the benefit within yourself. You also realize at that time that anyone could do this, anyone could have this same experience, this same realization, and derive the same benefit, because all beings have the same nature of the mind. Since all beings could experience this same realization and benefit – as they all possess the Buddha-essence – and yet do not experience it, and in not doing so, suffer tremendously, you are naturally touched or inspired to be compassionate. This seems to always go along with Mahamudra experience.

Question: Rinpoche, I wanted to ask about relaxing the mind, when you are looking at the mind. What is it exactly that relaxes, and is relaxing the mind somehow connected with merit and having merit to do that.

Rinpoche: The opposite of the type of relaxation that is being suggested here is a type of tension that is based upon fear, such as the thought, "I can't think, I mustn't think, I will not think, oh I thought, oh I stopped that thought, I did not stop that one, it slipped by," and so on. That type of attitude toward meditation turns the whole thing into a fight. What is meant by relaxation is an attitude toward meditation, and therefore a conduct of meditation, where, when thoughts arise, you just let them arise, and you look at them directly. It means less effort and also a different kind of attitude or environment for the practice. As for the relationship between the ability to relax in meditation and the accumulation of merit, the accumulation of merit is helpful in any aspect of meditation. It is always helpful, and that is why it is recommended that people have completed the preliminary practices (*Ngöndro*) before receiving the instructions on Mahamudra. By doing the prostrations you have increased your faith and devotion, which enhances your commitment and involvement with the practice. By doing the Vajrasattva practice, you have removed some of the tendencies that would cause uncontrolled thoughts to afflict you in practice. By performing the mandala offering, you have gathered the accumulations that make it more possible or workable for you to do the practice of Mahamudra, and by practicing guru-yoga you have received the guru's blessing, which brings experience and realization. All of these practices, which lead to the accumulations of merit and wisdom, are helpful in many ways in the practice of Mahamudra. However, you should not mistake these words to mean that someone who has not completed these practices cannot do Mahamudra practice. They can. It is just that these practices are very helpful.

Notes

1. The depiction of Tilopa holding a fish is based upon the story of Naropa's first meeting with Tilopa. When Naropa went to look for Tilopa he had no real idea where exactly he was. Naropa was just going on a prediction he had received that told him that the one who would be his guru, Tilopa, was somewhere in Eastern India and that his name was Tilop or Tilopa. He had no idea beyond that of what Tilopa looked like or exactly where he was. Therefore he had a lot of difficulty finding him. Having gone through a lot of difficulty already and still not having found him, one day he tracked him down to a certain locality, and when he arrived there, he asked the local people if the Mahasiddha Tilopa lived there. The person he spoke to said they had never heard of any Mahasiddha Tilopa, but that there was a beggar Tilopa who was right over there, indicating a place nearby. Naropa was inspired by this because he thought Tilopa was a mahasiddha, and therefore he could be living as a beggar. What he saw when he went over to meet Tilopa for the first time was Tilopa sitting there with a pile of fish that he had caught, snapping his fingers and thereby causing the consciousness of each fish to be liberated into the dharmadhatu, after which he would eat the fish. As this was the first one of Tilopa's more famous recorded miraculous displays, and was the first occasion when Naropa actually came into his physical presence, it is commemorated by the traditional depiction of Tilopa holding a fish. – *Thrangu Rinpoche*
2. These six special yogic practices were transmitted from Naropa to Marpa and consist of the subtle heat practice, the illusory body practice, the dream yoga practice, the luminosity practice, the ejection of consciousness practice and the bardo practice.
3. The deities Chakrasamvara, Vajrayogini, and Chenrezig are not individual

entities that are like living beings. The best way to understand them is to see them as dharmata, the completely vast state of emptiness which is replete with the guru's wisdom and has extreme power and luminosity. The very nature of this luminosity is compassion. There is a huge amount of power in the completely even and empty space of dharmata. That power is such that without any particular intention or direction by any kind of thought, it will manifest to benefit sentient beings in a myriad of different ways. This could be as Chakrasamvara, Vajrayogini, or as a king, an animal, a queen, or a beggar. The power of this luminosity and compassion is such that without making some sort of decision like, "I will manifest in this way to benefit so and so" it just happens spontaneously. This is how we may understand the nature of these deities. They are arisen from the power of luminosity and compassion of the Buddha nature which is emptiness – dharmata itself. – *Thrangu Rinpoche*

4. Fully enlightened beings, Buddhas, and their manifestations are often understood by way of the three kayas: The dharmakaya is enlightenment itself, wisdom beyond any reference point which can only be perceived by other enlightened beings; The sambhogakaya, often called the enjoyment body, manifests in the pure lands which can only be seen by advanced bodhisattvas; and the nirmanakaya which can be seen by ordinary beings as in the case of the historical Buddha, but this can also be any type of being or relative appearance to assist ordinary beings. The historical Buddha Shakyamuni lived in the fourth century before the birth of Christ (the current era or CE)

5. When you talk about guru in the Mahamudra lineage, there is the pure (dharmakaya) aspect of the guru, the distance lineage gurus, and the close lineage gurus. The distance lineage gurus start with the Lord Buddha and extend in a continuous, unbroken succession of enlightened masters and students all the way down to the Karmapa. We call that the distance lineage because it goes all the way back to the Buddha Shakyamuni.

There is the close lineage of Mahamudra as well. That lineage begins with the Buddha Vajradhara who bestowed Mahamudra teachings on the Bodhisattva Lodro Rinchen, which teachings then come down to Tilopa and Naropa. In the case of the great masters who received Mahamudra lineage transmissions directly from the Buddha Vajradhara, those transmissions happened a long time after Prince Siddhartha's paranirvana. The physical Buddha, the historical Buddha Shakyamuni, Prince Siddhartha, was at the time no longer in physical Prince Siddhartha form. What happened was that

Notes

first these great masters received the teachings of the Buddha and the Buddha's disciples through "distance lineages," and they practiced them. Through their practice they attained realization. As part of their realization the Buddha manifested to them, but not as Prince Siddhartha, as Buddha Vajradhara. So, Buddha, the sambhogakaya of the Buddha, and the nirmanakaya of the Buddha, which is Prince Siddhartha in our case. The Buddha Vajradhara means all in one – the ever present Buddha, the timeless Buddha.

Then the Buddha Vajradhara transmitted directly to certain great masters, but only as a result of the realization of the teachings they had already received from their masters, whose teachings started with the historical Buddha. In this way, the Mahamudra lineage and many Vajrayana Buddhist lineages actually have distance lineage as well as close lineage. – *Tai Situ Rinpoche*

6. Tilopa was different from the other Kagyu lineage holders such as Marpa and Milarepa in that Tilopa was an actual emanation of Chakrasamvara and could therefore have direct experience of Vajradhara. Marpa, in contrast, was an ordinary person who gained enlightenment through his practice. However Tilopa still had physical limitations due to his karmically conditioned body. An example is the *garuda* bird who is born with wings and has the power to fly, but is still contained in this fine envelope of the egg shell. In the same way, until that last egg shell of his karmically conditioned physical form is broken, the garuda can't fly. – *Thrangu Rinpoche*

7. It is generally accepted that Nagarjuna, the founder of Madhyamaka school, lived in the second century and Tilopa lived in the ninth century. Rinpoche says however that mahasiddhas, unlike ordinary beings, have the power to appear at different times and different places.

8. The display of miracles such as trees becoming warriors arises from the samadhi recognizing that all phenomena are uncreated and are, in fact, illusory. Whatever is required to benefit beings can be magically manifested out of the samadhi realizing this emptiness. – *Thrangu Rinpoche*

9. The "secret mantrayana" is another name for the Vajrayana.

10. The three heart spheres (Tib. *ning po kor sum*) are actually the title of a tantra called *The Mahamudra Tantra*.

11. The ultimate or supreme siddhi is the stable realisation of the radiant clarity or clear light nature of mind and all reality which we know as complete and perfect enlightenment or Buddhahood. The relative siddhis are such qualities as loving kindness, compassion, intelligence, the wisdom of insight, spiritual power, protection, the removal of obstacles, good health, longevity, wealth and magnetism etc. – *Lama Tashi Namgyal*

12. This *doha* is given in *The Rain of Wisdom*, Shambhala Publications, 1980 p. 126-128.
13. The Madhyamaka or Middle-way school is divided into two major schools by the Tibetans: the Rangtong school which follows the teachings of Nagarjuna fairly closely and maintains that everything is completely empty and the Shentong school which maintains that that this emptiness is indivisible from luminosity/clarity (Tib. *salwa*) and that all sentient beings possess Buddha-essence.
14. What is called "the western land of Urgyen" refers to the land of total enjoyment of the dakas and dakinis who have realized the profound levels of realization and mastery of phenomena. Urgyen refers here to a level of realization. However, it seems that there were a lot of mahasiddhas who came from a particular area in the western part of India and this place was called Urgyen. In the prayer to Padmasambhava it says, "You who have gone to the northwest border of Urgyen." There is a very symbolic meaning to these cardinal directions such as west so it is hard to locate this place literally. At the same time, the symbolical meanings are involved with actual directions as we think of them. – *Thrangu Rinpoche*
15. The first quality is having perfect samaya, the second is having received a command or prophecy of one's future enlightenment and the third is having a deep level of realization. Being an emanation himself is fulfilment of the second and third prophecies.
16. In the Vajrayana, there are two paths – *drol lam* and *thap lam* – that are generally followed simultaneously or alternately by the practitioner. *Drol lam,* the path of liberation, is what sometimes we refer to as formless meditation and includes Mahamudra. In this approach to meditation one relates to the mind in terms of the awareness aspect of mind.

Thap lam, the path of means or method, includes all tantric practices employing visualization, mantras, mandalas, yogas such as *the Six Dharmas of Naropa* or the *Six Dharmas of Niguma,* etc. These practices relate to mind in terms of the energy aspect of mind. By properly integrating the distorted karmic energies of one's mind, one brings about the same enlightened awareness that is reached as the fruition of the formless meditation approach of the path of liberation. The virtue of the path of liberation is that it tends to be smoother, while the path of means is that it tends to be faster; therefore, they make a good complement to each other. Neither path can be practiced properly – and in the case of the

path of means it would be dangerous to do so – without the guidance of a qualified tantric master. – *Lama Tashi Namgyal*
17. When Tilopa says, "I have the key of prophecy because I have realized Mahamudra" he is referring to instantaneous prophecy. The word "prophecy" in Tibetan is "*jung ten*" which means prediction and there are two kinds of prophecy. The first is when an individual says, "In the future time so and so will attain such and such state of realization." The other kind of prophecy is when an individual through direct experience knows something and has attained something. That is what is being referred to as the instantaneous understanding of having attained Mahamudra. – *Thrangu Rinpoche*
18. Naropa's biography and teachings have been taught in English by Chogyam Trungpa Rinpoche and published as *Illusion's Game, The Life and Teaching of Naropa*, available from Shambhala Publications.
19. Previously in the time of the Buddha when taking refuge the hair of the disciple was shaved. Presently, just a lock of hair is usually cut.
20. There are the three higher realms of existence – the human, the jealous god and the god realms. These realms are superior in that the beings in these realms don't have to experience a great deal of pain and suffering. They do experience degrees of happiness and joy because of their previous virtuous actions. These states are still part of samsara and beings in them still maintain their clinging to ideas of reality and haven't dissolved them by realizing that all phenomena are uncreated. In the god realm, for example, beings are so distracted by their experience of pleasure that they have no inclination to gain liberation. Unlike the human realm where we have moments of satisfaction, in the god realm there is a continual craving and continual gratification of that craving. However, there are many beings in the god realm who do practice the dharma and are not totally bewildered by their experience of pleasure and can practice the dharma. – *Thrangu Rinpoche*
21. *Moonbeams of Mahamudra* is a text by Dagpo Tashi Namgyal which outlines in great detail the entire path of Mahamudra. It has been translated by Lhalungpa and published as *Mahamudra: The Quintessence of Mind and Meditation*, Shambhala Publications. Thrangu Rinpoche has given an extensive commentary on this work and these are published in the two volume work: *Looking Directly at Mind: The Moonlight of Mahamudra*. Namo Buddha Publications.
22. Disturbing emotions are kleshas which in Sanskrit means "pain, distress, and torment." This was translated as "afflictions" which is the closest

English word to what causes distress. However, the Tibetan word for kleshas is *nyon mong* and these almost always refer to passion, anger, ignorance, jealousy, and pride which are actually negative or disturbing emotions so we prefer the translation negative or disturbing emotion since "afflictions" imply some kind of disability. *The Great Tibetan Dictionary* for example defines *nyon mong* as, "mental events that incite one to non-virtuous actions and cause one's being to be very unpeaceful."

23. In the East, as in classical times, it was thought that the mind resides in the heart rather than the brain. This is why when we say "in my heart" or "heartfelt" we are referring to emotions and strong thoughts.
24. A free and well favoured situation is to be born with eight freedoms and ten opportunities (*Tal jor*). *Tal* is often translated as "freedom" and *jor* as "endowments," "qualities," "resources," or "opportunities" which constitute a precious human birth to practice dharma. The eight freedoms are traditionally enumerated as freedom from birth as a hell being, a hungry ghost, an animal, a barbarian, a long-lived god, a heretic, a mentally handicapped person, or living in a dark age (here meaning when no Buddha has come; in other contexts, according to the teachings on five degenerations we are living in a dark age). Of the ten conjunctions or resources, the five personal conjunctions are having a human body, being born in a land to which the dharma has spread, having all of one's senses intact, not reverting to evil ways, and having confidence in the three jewels. (Having one's senses impaired to the extent that one's mind could not function properly in the study and practice of dharma would constitute the loss of one's precious human birth.) The five conjunctions that come by way of others are that a Buddha has been born in this age, that the Buddha taught the dharma, that the dharma still exists, that there are still followers who have realized the meaning and essence of the teachings of the dharma, and there are benevolent sponsors. – *Lama Tashi Namgyal*
25. This is the translation of the Tibetan word *salwa* which is also translated variously as "brilliance," "luminous clarity," and "luminosity." We must not make the mistake of thinking of this as some kind of light such as we get from a light bulb even though the words suggest this. Rather it is simply that continuous awareness, that knowing, that the mind always has.
26. What is here being translated as "conduct," in many of Chogyam Trungpa Rinpoche's teachings and translations is translated as "action." – *Lama Tashi Namgyal*

Notes

27. The five-fold posture is: first that the body should be "as straight as an arrow," which means the back should be straight and not leaning; second, the chin should be bent slightly inward like a hook; the third point is that the legs should be crossed (full lotus is best or else half lotus); fourth is that the body "should be gathered together like chains," which means lock it in position as with iron shackles, the way to do this is to join the hands, placing them the width of four fingers below the navel; fifth is to keep one's mind and body reasonably tight, exerting a certain amount of effort so the body and mind are composed and focused.

    This is the preferred posture of Marpa, who said if one can keep the body in this posture, the subtle energy circulating in the body would be ideal and would then actually circulate through the central channel of the body. – *Thrangu Rinpoche*

28. The first recognition of the nature of mind, which is brought about in the student's experience through the intervention of the lama – whether during a teaching, a ritual ceremony, or guided meditation – becomes the basis for the student's subsequent practice of dharma, the purpose of which is to enable the student to become accustomed and habituated to experiencing the world in the manner first pointed out. When through the practice of the path, the student's experience reaches the ineffable fruition of Buddhahood, he or she is said to have fully realized the nature of mind. – *Lama Tashi Namgyal*

29. The word "look" is used here, but clearly this has nothing to do with sight. The word is used to contrast it with analyzing or examining which has an analytical, cognitive component which isn't present in "looking" at mind. So looking at mind implies direct and non-conceptual examination.

30. If you have studied a great deal, and in particular have studied the *Madhyamakavatara* by Chandrakirti and the *Bodhicharyavatara* by Shantideva, such as the ninth chapter in [the latter] text on prajna, then you will have encountered the statement that it is impossible for the mind to be aware of itself. This is taught in the Madhyamaka system in these texts, and many reasons are given for this statement. Khenchen Thrangu Rinpoche, makes the following comments on this seeming discrepancy. "Here what is being given in these texts is a refutation of substantialist schools who assert that a substantial mind can see its substantial self in the way that our physical eye actually sees something, a visual form, that appears to be out there" These Madhyamika texts do not contradict the Mahamudra meditation and view, "Because what is being discussed in

Chandrakirti's and Shantideva's writings is the substantialist notion that a substantial or truly existing mind can see itself as a substantially existent thing." And that is correctly refuted as impossible. In the Mahamudra practice, "We are talking about a mind of which the fundamental nature is emptiness, and of which the primary characteristic is cognitive lucidity, looking at itself and seeing its own emptiness, and through being aware of that emptiness, recognizing its own cognitive lucidity, which is entirely different from a substantial thing seeing itself."

31. Latencies (Skt. *vasana*, Tib. *bakchak*) These latent imprints that enter the eighth consciousness come through the seventh consciousness. These imprints are not apparently the experience itself, but are described more like dormant seeds which are away from soil, water, and sunlight. These imprints are either positive, negative, or neutral depending upon whether they came from a positive, negative, or neutral thought or action. These imprints are then activated with experience and thus help create our impression of the solidity of the world. There are actually several kinds of latencies: latencies which are associated with external sensory experiences, latencies which give rise to the dualistic belief of "I" and "other," and positive and negative latencies due to our actions which cause us to continue to revolve around and around in samsara.

    It should also be pointed out that different schools of Buddhism treated these latencies differently. The Mind-only school of the Cittamatrins founded by Asanga in the fourth century B.C.E holds that there are eight consciousnesses and the latencies are responsible for us remaining in samsara and also experiencing the world as solid and not empty. The Madhyamaka followers of the Sautrantika school hold that there is an objective external reality and that there are only seven consciousnesses and therefore no eighth consciousness. Basically they believe that the seventh consciousness receives these latencies and projects the outside world. The Madhyamaka followers of the Prasangika school do not hold that there is an external reality and say that there is no seventh or eighth consciousness. They posit that the self is a conceptual stream that receives these latencies and is involved in the projection of external phenomena. The subject of different schools is, of course, extremely more complicated that this and there are presentday sects which adhere to one or another of these views.

32. The failure of the mind to recognize its own true nature is what is meant by the term *ma rigpa*, or ignorance, the first level of obscuration or

defilement in the mind. As a result of this ignorance, there arises in the mind the imputation of an "I" and an "other," (the other being something that is conceived as) something that is other than the mind. This dualistic clinging, something that we have had throughout beginningless time and that never stops (until enlightenment), is the second level of obscuration, the obscuration of habits (habitual tendency).

Based upon this dualistic clinging arise the three root mental afflictions: mental darkness (variously rendered by translators as ignorance, bewilderment, confusion, etc.), desire, and aggression. Based upon these three afflictions there arise some 84,000 various mental afflictions enumerated by the Buddha, all of which together comprise the third level of obscuration, called the obscuration of mental afflictions (variously rendered as *klesha*, emotional affliction, conflicting emotions, etc). Under the influence of these, we perform actions that are obscured in their nature, which result in the fourth level of obscuration, called the obscuration of actions or karma. – *Khabje Kalu Rinpoche*

33. Selflessness, in the writings of Chogyam Trungpa Rinpoche, is called egolessness. One-fold egolessness is the equivalent of the selflessness of persons. One-and-a-half-fold egolessness is the selflessness of persons plus the lack of inherent existence of phenomena; while two-fold egolessness is the selflessness of persons, the lack of inherent existence of phenomena, plus the lack of inherent existence of consciousness. In Thrangu Rinpoche's rendering here, the selflessness of dharmas – phenomena – includes both halves of the second fold of egolessness. The view presented by Trungpa Rinpoche was the view of Maitreya, and hence belongs to the Shentong view; whereas, in the context of analytical meditation it is presented by way of the Rangtong view of Masters Nagarjuna and Chandrakirti. In the latter view, since phenomena exist only in dependence upon the consciousness that perceive them, and consciousness exists only in dependence on the phenomena they perceive, it is nonsensical to discuss or categorize them as though they were independent entities.

34. Blessing is the process by which one individual introduces some of their accumulated merit into another's "stream of being." The ability to bestow blessing depends on the donor's degree of spiritual attainment and on the recipient's faith. The donor is usually the root-guru, whose blessing is said to contain that of all the sources of refuge combined. Although future experiences are largely shaped by present actions, the root-guru's blessing can partially modify this. That is, it can create conditions favourable to

the maturation of any religious pre-dispositions our past actions may have generated, giving us the inspiration and energy we require to begin practicing. In this way, unless our acts have been extremely unwholesome, the guru's blessing can help us overcome conflicting emotions and other obstacles. Thus the guru's blessing helps us realize the Buddha-potential we all possess.

35. The Kagyu lineage supplication, called the Dorje Chang Tungma in Tibetan is recited in almost all Kagyu centers throughout the world on a daily basis. Thrangu Rinpoche has written an extensive commentary on this Prayer in *Showing the Path to Liberation*. Namo Buddha & Zhyisil Chokyi Ghatsal Publications.

36. In Tibet there were two periods of the introduction of Buddhism. The initial or first period of the spread of the teachings occurred in the 8th and 9th centuries in what is now known as the Nyingma or old tradition. The second period occurred during the 11th century with new translations from India and this led to what is called the Sarma traditions which include the Kagyu, Sakya and Gelugpa schools.

37. There are three main traditions in Buddhism: Hinayana, Mahayana, and Vajrayana. While Tibetan Buddhists actually practice all three levels, Tibet is one of the few traditionally Buddhist countries which practice the Vajrayana.

38. For a detailed explanation of this see, Thrangu Rinpoche's *Transcending Ego: Distinguishing Consciousness from Wisdom*. Namo Buddha Publications.

39. All meditation can be divided into the two categories of tranquillity meditation (Shamatha) and insight meditation (Vipashyana). Vipashyana in turn can be divided into the Vipashyana of the sutra tradition and the Vipashyana of the Mahamudra tradition. In the sutra tradition there is analytical Vipashyana and placement meditation. In the Mahamudra or tantric tradition, Vipashyana is based on the direct pointing out of the nature of mind and the nature of things by a fully qualified and experienced holder of the Mahamudra lineage. – *Lama Tashi Namgyal*

Glossary of Terms

84,000 (classes of dharma) teachings. (Tib. *cho kyi phung po gyad khri bzhi stong*) 21,000 teachings on each of the Vinaya, Sutra, Abhidharma, and their combination. Their purpose is to eliminate the 84,000 different types of disturbing emotions latent in one's mind.

Abhidharma. (Tib. *chö ngön pa*) The Buddhist teachings are often divided into the Tripitaka: the sutras (teachings of the Buddha), the Vinaya (teachings on conduct,) and the Abhidharma which are the analyses of phenomena that exist primarily as a commentarial tradition to the Buddhist teachings.

Abhidharmakaosha. (Tib. *ngön pa dzod*) An authoritative scripture on Buddhist metaphysics according to the Hinayana tradition.

Absolute truth. (Tib. *dondam*) There are two truths or views of reality – relative truth which is seeing things as ordinary beings do with the dualism of "I" and "other" and ultimate truth, which transcends duality and sees things as they are.

Amrita. (Tib. *dut tsi*) A blessed substance which can cause spiritual and physical healing.

Arhat. "Free from four maras." The mara of conflicting emotions, the mara of the deva, the mara of death and the mara of the skandhas. The highest level of the Hinayana path. Arhat is male and arhati is female.

Arhatship. The stage of having fully eliminated the klesha obscurations.

Asanga. (Tib. *thok may*) A fourth century Indian philosopher who founded the Cittamatra or Yogacara school and wrote the five works of Maitreya which are important mahayana works. Also brother of Vasubandhu.

Atisha. (982-1055 C.E.) A Buddhist scholar at University in India who came to Tibet at the invitation of the King to overcome the damage done by Langdarma. He helped found the Kadampa tradition.

Avalokiteshvara. (Tib. *Chenrezig*) The bodhisattva embodying the compassion of all the Buddhas. Depicted holding the wish-fulfilling gem between folded hands. One of the eight main bodhisattvas. The mantra associated with this bodhisattva is known as the king of mantras, OM MANI PEME HUNG.

Ayatanas. These are the six sensory objects of sight, sound, smell, taste, and body sensation; the six sense faculties, the visual sensory faculty, the auditory sensory faculty, etc., and the six sensory consciousnesses, the visual consciousness, the auditory consciousness, etc. They make up the eighteen constituents for perception.

Bardo. (Tib.) The intermediate state between the end of one life and rebirth into another. Bardo can also be divided into six different levels; the bardo of birth, dreams, meditation, the moment before death, the bardo of dharmata and the bardo of becoming.

Bhikshu. (Tib. *ge long*) A fully ordained monk.

Bindu. (Tib. *tigle*) Vital essence drops or spheres of psychic energy that are often visualized in Vajrayana practices.

Blessings. (Tib. chin lap) Splendour wave, conveying the sense of atmosphere descending or coming toward the practitioner. One's root guru and lineage are said to be the source of blessings. When the student can open themselves with uncontrived devotion, the grace of the lineage manifests as blessings, which dissolve into them and awaken them to a sense of greater reality.

The process by which one individual introduces some of their accumulated merit into another's "stream of being." The ability to bestow blessing depends on the donor's degree of spiritual attainment and on the recipient's faith. The donor is usually the root-guru, whose blessing is said to contain that of all the sources of refuge combined. Although future experiences are largely shaped by present actions, the root-guru's blessing can partially modify this. That is, it can create conditions favourable to the maturation of any religious predispositions our past actions may have generated, giving us the inspiration and energy we require to begin practising. In this way, unless our acts have been extremely unwholesome, the guru's blessing can help us overcome conflicting emotions and other obstacles. Thus the guru's blessing helps us realize the Buddha-potential we all possess.

Bodhi tree. The pipil tree that Buddha achieved enlightenment under. It is the *ficus religiousus.*

Bodhichitta. (Tib. *chang chup chi sem*) Literally, the mind of enlightenment. There are two kinds of bodhichitta: absolute bodhichitta, which is completely awakened mind that sees the emptiness of phenomena, and relative bodhichitta which is the aspiration to practice the six paramitas and free all beings from the suffering of samsara. In regard to relative bodhichitta there is also two kinds: aspiration bodhichitta and perseverance bodhichitta.

Bodhisattva. (Tib. *chang chup sem pa*) "Heroic mind." *Bodhi* means blossomed or enlightened, and *sattva* means heroic mind. Literally, one who exhibits the mind of enlightenment. Also an individual who has committed him or herself to the Mahayana path of compassion and the practice of the six paramitas to achieve buddhahood to free all beings from samsara. These are the heart or mind disciples of the Buddha.

Bodhisattva levels. (Skt. *bhumi,* Tib. *sa*) The levels or stages a bodhisattva goes through to reach enlightenment. These consist of ten levels in the sutra tradition and thirteen in the tantra tradition.

Bodhisattva vow. The vow to attain buddhahood for the sake of all beings.

Buddha. (Tib. *sang gye*) An individual who attains, or the attainment of, complete enlightenment, such as the historical Shakyamuni Buddha.

Buddha Shakyamuni. (Tib. *shakya tubpa*) The Shakyamuni Buddha, often called the Gautama Buddha, refers to the fourth Buddha of this age, who lived between 563 and 483 BCE.

Buddhafield. (Tib. *sang gye kyi zhing*) 1) One of the realms of the five Buddha families, either as sambhogakaya or nirmanakaya. 2) Pure personal experience.

Buddhahood. (Tib. *sang gyas*) The perfect and complete enlightenment of dwelling in neither samsara nor nirvana. Expression of the realization of perfect enlightenment, which characterizes a Buddha. The attainment of buddhahood is the birthright of all beings. According to the teachings of Buddha, every sentient being has, or better is already, buddha nature; thus buddhahood cannot be "attained." It is much more a matter of experiencing the primordial perfection and realizing it in everyday life.

Buddha-essence. (Tib. *de shegs nying po*) The essential nature of all sentient beings. The potential for enlightenment.

Chakra. A complex systematic description of physical and psychological energy channels.

Chakrasamvara. (Tib. *korlo dompa*) A meditational deity which belongs to the Anuttarayoga tantra set of teachings. A main yidam or tantra of the New Schools.

Chandrakirti. A seventh century Indian Buddhist scholar of the Madhyamaka school who is best known for founding the Prasangika subschool and writing two treatises on emptiness using logical reasoning.

Channels, winds and essences. Nadi, prana and bindu; the constituents of the vajra body. These channels are not anatomical structures, but more like meridians in acupuncture. There are thousands of channels, but the three main channels that carry the subtle energy are the right, left and central channel. The central channel runs roughly along the spinal column while the right and left are on the sides of the central channel.

According to the yogic teachings of the path of skilful means, realization is attained through synchronization of body and mind. This may be achieved through meditating on nadi (channels), prana (energy), and bindu (drops) — the psychic components in the illusory body. Prana is the energy, or "wind," moving through the nadis. As is said, "Mind consciousness rides the horse of prana on the pathways of the nadis. The bindu is mind's nourishment."

Because of dualistic thinking, prana enters the left and right channels. This divergence of energy in the illusory body corresponds to the mental activity that falsely distinguishes between subject and object and leads to karmically determined activity. Through yogic practice, the pranas can be brought into the central channel and therefore transformed into wisdom-prana. Then the mind can recognize its fundamental nature, realizing all dharmas as unborn.

This belongs to advanced practice and can only be learned through direct oral transmission from an accomplished guru. Once the meditator is well established in the experience of the fundamental nature of mind, they can meditate on it directly, dissolving the nadi, prana, and bindu visualization. Meditation using the concept of psychic channels is regarded as being the completion stage with signs, and the formless practice which contemplates the nature of mind directly is the completion stage without signs

Chittamatra school. (Tib. *sem tsampa*) A school founded by Asanga in the fourth century and is usually translated as the Mind-only school. It is one of the four major schools in the Mahayana tradition and its main tenet (to greatly simplify) is that all phenomena are mental events.

Chöd. (Tib.) This is pronounced "chö" and literally means "to cut off" and refers to a practice that is designed to cut off all ego involvement and defilements. The *mo chöd* (female chöd) practice was founded by the famous female saint Machig Labdron (1031 to 1129 C. E.).

Clarity. (Tib. *salwa*) Also translated as luminosity. The nature of mind is that it is empty of inherent existence, but the mind is not just voidness or completely empty because it has this clarity which is awareness or the knowing of mind. So clarity is a characteristic of emptiness (*shunyata*) of mind.

Co-emergent wisdom. (Skt. *sahajajnana*, Tib. *lhen chik kye pay yeshe*) The advanced realization of the inseparability of samsara and nirvana and how these arise simultaneously and together.

Cognizance. (Tib. *selwa*) The mind's inherent capacity for knowing.

Commentary. (Skt. *shastra*, Tib. *tan chö*) The Buddhist teachings are divided into the words of the Buddha (*sutras*) and the commentaries of others on his works (*shastras*).

Completion stage. (Tib. *dzo rim*) In the Vajrayana there are two stages of meditation: the creation/development stage and the completion stage. Completion stage with marks is the six doctrines. Completion stage without marks is the practice of essence Mahamudra, resting in the unfabricated nature of mind.

Consciousnesses, eight (Skt. *vijñana*, Tib. *nam she tsog gye*) The eight consciousnesses consist of the five sense consciousnesses: sight, sound, smell, taste and tactile consciousne, all of which are non-conceptual. The remaining three are: the sixth is the mental consciousness which thinks and discriminates between good and bad and is thus said to be "with thought"; the seventh is known as the "afflicted or klesha consciousness," which refers to the most subtle level of mental affliction, specifically the subtle and unfluctuatingly present fixation on a self, it continues until attainment of the first bodhisattva level: the eighth is called "the ground consciousness" or "all-basis consciousness" which is the foundation or basis for the arising of all the other consciousnesses and stores the habitual patterns accumulated through physical and mental activities. Like the seventh it is constantly present and operating. It persists until the final attainment of Buddhahood. For a detailed explanation of these consciousnesses see Thrangu Rinpoche's book, *Transcending Ego: Distinguishing Consciousness from Wisdom.* Namo Buddha Publications.

Conventional truth. (Tib. *kundzop*) There are two truths: relative and absolute or ultimate truth. Relative truth is the perception of an ordinary (unenlightened) being who sees the world with all his or her projections based on the false belief in "I" and "other."

Creation stage. (Skt. *utpattikrama*, Tib. *che rim*) In the Vajrayana there are two stages of meditation: the development and the completion stage. The creation stage is a method of tantric meditation that involves the visualization and contemplation of deities for the purpose of purifying habitual tendencies and realizing the purity of all phenomena. In this stage visualization of the deity is established and maintained.

Daka. (Tib. *khandro*) A male counterpart to a dakini.

Dakini. (Tib. *khandroma*) A yogini who has attained high realizations of the fully enlightened mind. She may be a human being who has achieved such attainments or a non-human manifestation of the enlightened mind of a meditational deity. A female aspect of the protectors. It is feminine energy which has inner, outer and secret meanings.

Definitive meaning. The Buddha's teachings that state the direct meaning of dharma. They are not changed or simplified for the capacity of the listener, in contrast to the provisional meaning.

Desire realm. Comprises the six realms of gods, demi-gods, humans, animals, hungry spirits and hell-beings.

Dharani. A particular type of mantra, usually quite long.

Dharma. (Tib. *chö*) This has two main meanings: first, any truth, such as that the sky is blue; and secondly, the teachings of the Buddha (also called "Buddha-dharma").

Dharmadhatu. (Tib. *chö ying*) The all-encompassing space, unoriginated and without beginning, out of which all phenomena arises. The Sanskrit means "the essence of phenomena" and the Tibetan means "the expanse of phenomena," but it usually refers to the emptiness that is the essence of phenomena.

Dharmakaya. (Tib. *chö ku*) One of the three bodies of buddhahood. It is enlightenment itself, that is, wisdom beyond any point of reference. (see *kayas, three.*)

Dharmata. (Tib. *chö nyi*) Dharmata is often translated as "suchness" or "the true nature of things" or "things as they are." It is phenomena as it really is or as seen by a completely enlightened being without any distortion or obscuration, so one can say it is "reality." The nature of phenomena and mind.

Disturbing emotions. (Skt. *klesha*, Tib. *nyön mong*) Also called the "afflictive emotions," these are the emotional afflictions or obscurations (in contrast to intellectual obscurations) that disturb the clarity of perception. These are also translated as "poisons." They include any emotion that disturbs or distorts consciousness. The main kleshas are desire, anger and ignorance.

Doha. (Tib. *gur*) A spiritual song spontaneously composed by a Vajrayana practitioner. It usually has nine syllables per line.

Dzogchen. (Skt. *mahasandhi*) Literally "the great perfection" The teachings beyond the vehicles of causation, first taught in the human world by the great vidyadhara Garab Dorje.

Eight consciousnesses. The all-ground consciousness, mind-consciousness, afflicted consciousness, and the five sense-consciousnesses. The Hinayana sutras generally discuss mind in terms of six consciousnesses, namely, the five sensory consciousnesses and the sixth mental consciousness. The Mahayana Cittamatra school (Mind-only) school talks about the eight consciousness in which the first six are the same but has the seventh and eighth consciousnesses added. In the Hinayana tradition the functions of the seventh and eighth consciousness are subsumed in the sixth mental consciousness.

Eight fold noble path. Right view, right thought, right speech, right action, right livelihood, right effort, right mindfulness and right concentration.

Eight worldly concerns. (Tib. *jik ten chö gysh*) These keep one from the path; they are attachment to gain, attachment to pleasure, attachment to praise, attachment to fame, aversion to loss, aversion to pain, aversion to blame and aversion to a bad reputation.

Empowerment. (Tib. *wang* Skt. *abhiseka*) The conferring of power or authorization to practice the Vajrayana teachings, the indispensable entrance door to tantric practice. To do a Vajrayana practice one must receive the empowerment from a qualified lama. One should also receive the practice instruction (Tib. *tri*) and the textual reading (Tib. *lung*).

Emptiness. (Tib. *tong pa nyi* Skt. *shunyata*) A central theme in Buddhism. It should not lead one to views of nihilism or the like, but is a term indicating the lack of any truly existing independent nature of any and all phenomena. Positively stated, phenomena do exist, but as mere appearances, interdependent manifestations of mind with no limitation. It is not that it is just your mind, as mind is also free of any true existence. This frees one from a solipsist view. This is interpreted differently by the individual schools.

Enlightenment. (Skt. *bodhi* Tib. *jang chub*) According to the Buddhadharma, theistic and mystical experiences of all kinds still fall within samsara, as long as they confirm the experiencer or solidify the experience, even in the most subtle way. Buddhist norms of experience are: universal impermanence, existence as suffering, selflessness, and peace as absence of struggle to attain or maintain anything.

The Hinayana tradition defines enlightenment as the cessation of ignorance and of conflicting emotions, and therefore freedom from the compulsive rebirth in samsara. Its degrees of attainment were enumerated as four levels: stream enterer, once returner, non-returner and arhat.

According to the Mahayana tradition, Hinayana nirvana is a way station, like an illusory city in the desert created by the Buddha to encourage travellers. Enlightenment requires not only cessation of ignorance but also compassion and skilful means to work with the bewilderment of all sentient beings. The arhat does not attain complete enlightenment because of their undeveloped compassion.

According to the Vajrayana tradition, Hinayana and Mahayana attainment are necessary, but they contain dogma. It is necessary for the yogin to develop complete partnership with the phenomenal world and to experience a more penetrating unmasking of the root of ego. In presenting the final fruition, the Vajrayana teaches either four or six yanas.

The term nirvana can have the utmost positive sense when referring to enlightenment; or it can have a limiting or pejorative sense when referring to a limited goal of cessation.

Eternalism. (Tib. *rtag lta*) The belief that there is a permanent and causeless creator of everything; in particular, that one's identity or consciousness has a concrete essence which is independent, everlasting and singular.

Experience and realization. (Tib. *nyam togs*) An expression used for insight and progress on the path. "Experience" refers to temporary meditation experiences and "realization" to unchanging understanding of the nature of things.

Father tantra. (Tib. *pha gyu*) There are three kinds of tantras. The *father tantra* is concerned with transforming aggression, the *mother tantra* with transforming passion, and the *non-dual tantra* with transforming ignorance,

Five actions of immediate consequence. Killing one's father, killing one's mother, killing an arhat, intentionally wounding a Buddha and causing them to bleed, and creating a schism in the sangha. They are called actions which have an immediate result in that they are the cause for one's very next rebirth to be in a lower realm.

Five Buddha families. (Tib. *rig nga*) These are the Buddha, Vajra, Ratna, Padma and Karma families.

Five dhyani Buddhas. Vairochana, Akshobhya, Ratnasambhava, Amitabha and Amoghasiddhi. They are the pure aspects of the five elements and five emotions.

Five paths. (Tib. *lam nga*) According to the sutras there are five paths; the path of accumulation, the path of integration/junction, the path of seeing/insight, (attainment of the first bodhisattva level), the path of meditation, and the path of no more learning (Buddhahood). The five paths cover the entire process from beginning dharma practice to complete enlightenment.

Five wisdoms. The dharmadhatu wisdom, mirror-like wisdom, wisdom of equality, discriminating wisdom and all-accomplishing wisdom. They should not be understood as separate entities but rather as different functions of one's enlightened essence.

Fixation. (Tib. *dzin pa*) The mental act of holding on to a material object, experience, concept or set of philosophical ideas.

Form realm. God realms of subtle form.

Formless realm. (Tib. *zug med kyi kham*) The abode of an unenlightened being who has practiced the four absorptions of: infinite space, infinite consciousness, nothing whatsoever, and neither presence nor absence (of conception).

Four common preliminaries. The four ordinary foundations: the difficulty in obtaining the precious human body; impermanence and death; karma, cause and effect; the shortcomings of samsara. Reflection on these four reminders causes the mind to change and become directed toward the dharma.

Four empowerments. (Tib. *wang shi*) The empowerments of vase, secret, wisdom-knowledge and precious word.

Four extremes (Tib. *tha shi*) Existence, non-existence, both and neither.

Four immeasurables. Love, compassion, emphatic joy, and impartiality.

Four uncommon preliminaries. Refers to the four general preliminaries which are the four thoughts that turn the mind and the four special preliminaries which are the four practices of prostrations, Vajrasattva recitation, mandala offering and guru yoga.

Four seals. The four main principles of Buddhism: all compounded phenomena are impermanent, everything defiled (with ego-clinging) is suffering, all phenomena are empty and devoid of a self-entity, and nirvana is perfect peace.

Four thoughts. See four common preliminaries.

Four truths. The Buddha's first teachings. 1) All conditioned life is suffering. 2) All suffering is caused by ignorance. 3) Suffering can cease. 4) The eight-fold path leads to the end of suffering: right understanding, thought, speech, action, livelihood, effort, mindfulness and meditation.

Four Yogas of Mahamudra. (Tib. *phyag chen gyi nal byor zhi*) Four stages in Mahamudra practice: one-pointedness, simplicity, one taste and non-meditation.

Gampopa. (1079-1153 C.E.) One of the main lineage holders of the Kagyu lineage in Tibet. A student of Milarepa he established the first Kagyu monastic monastery and is known also for writing the *Jewel Ornament of Liberation.*

Ganachakra. (Tib. *tog kyi kor lo*) This is a ritual feast offering which is part of a spiritual practice.

Gandharva. (Tib. *dri za*) A class of deities that live of smells. They are also celestial musicians.

Garuda (Tib. *khyung*) A mythical bird that hatches fully grown.

Gelug school. One of the main four Tibetan schools of Buddhism founded by Tsong Khapa (1357-1419 C.E.) and is headed by His Holiness the fourteenth Dalai Lama.

Geshe. (Tib.) A scholar who has attained a doctorate in Buddhist studies. This usually takes fifteen to twenty years to attain.

Graded path. This refers to being guided through the path to enlightenment through the three principle paths, 1) renunciation, 2) enlightened motive of bodhicitta, 3) and a correct understanding of emptiness (wisdom).

Great bliss. (Skt. *mahasukha*, Tib. *deba chenpo*) A term for the quality of the experience of selflessness in Mahamudra tantra. Ultimate non-dualistic wisdom (Skt. *jnana*) is beyond ego and so there is no entity to experience the freedom of this state. Nevertheless, one can speak of the quality of this experience without an experiencer because it is not a blank state of mind. According to the teachings of Mahamudra, ego is actually a sort of filter that stands between the mind and the world. When this filter is removed, experience becomes so rich that it is as if ego has been intoxicated beyond its ordinary limitations and experiences the greater bliss, which is of another order and is beyond pleasure and pain. Thus, in a sense, great

Glossary of Terms

bliss is the unrecognized quality of all consciousness, whether dualistic or freed.

Guru. (Tib. *lama*) A teacher in the Tibetan tradition who has reached realization.

Guru-yoga. (Tib. *lamay naljor*) A practice of devotion to the guru culminating in receiving his blessing and blending indivisibly with his mind. Also refers to the fourth practice of the preliminary practices of ngöndro.

Guhyasamaja tantra. (Tib. *sang pa dus pa*) Literally, "Assembly of Secrets." One of the major tantras and yidams of the New School. This is the "father tantra" of the Anuttarayoga, which is the highest of the four tantras. Guhyasamaja is the central deity of the vajra family.

Hagiography. Combination of Greek *hagios* saint(ly) and *-graphy* writing of saints lives.

Heruka. (Tib. *trak thung*) A wrathful male deity.

Heart sutra. (Skt. *Mahaprajnaparamita-hridaya-sutra*) One of the shorter sutras on emptiness.

Hevajra. (Tib. *kye dorje*) This is the "mother tantra" of the Anuttarayoga tantra, which is the highest of the four yogas. "He" is said to be an exclamation of joy. Hevajra transforms sense pleasures into joy through the realization of the identity of form and emptiness. He is depicted in two, four, six, twelve, and sixteen-armed forms, dancing in union with his consort, usually Nairatmya.

Hevajra tantra. (Tib. *kye dorje*) This is the "mother tantra" of the Anuttarayoga tantra, which is the highest of the four yogas.

Higher realms. The three higher realms are birth as a human, demi-god and god.

Hinayana. (Tib. *tek pa chung wa*) Literally, the "lesser vehicle." The first of the three *yanas*, or vehicles. The term refers to the first teachings of the Buddha, which emphasized the careful examination of mind and its confusion. It is the foundation of Buddha's teachings focusing mainly on the four truths and the twelve interdependent links. The fruit is liberation for oneself.

Idiot compassion. This is the desire to help others but it is not accompanied by sufficient wisdom, so that what one does may not really be beneficial. An example is teaching someone who is hungry to fish, yet the person receives negative karma for killing the fish.

Illusory body (Tib. *gyu lu*) The transformation of a practitioner's very subtle energy body into a deathless miracle body of the deity during the completion stages. When this is purified it becomes the form body of the Buddha, one of the Six Yogas of Naropa. (see *Six Yogas of Naropa*)

Interdependent origination. The twelve links of causal connections which binds beings to samsaric existence and thus perpetuate suffering: ignorance, karmic formation, consciousness, name and form, the six sense bases, contact, sensation, craving, grasping, becoming, rebirth, old age, and death. These twelve links are like an uninterrupted vicious circle, a wheel that spins all sentient beings around and around through the realms of samsara.

Jnana. (Tib. *yeshe*) Enlightened wisdom that is beyond dualistic thought.

Jnanasattva. Skt. *Jnana* is awareness and *sattva* means mind.

Kadampa. (Tib.) One of the major schools in Tibet, it was founded by Atisha (993-1054 C.E.).

Kanjur. The preserved collection of the direct teaching of the Buddha.

Kagyu (Tib.) *Ka* means oral and *gyu* means lineage; The lineage of oral transmission. One of the four major schools of Buddhism in Tibet. It was founded in Tibet by Marpa and is headed by His Holiness Karmapa. The other three are the Nyingma, the Sakya and the Gelugpa schools.

Kalachakra. A tantra and a Vajrayana system taught by Buddha Shakyamuni.

Kalpa (Tib. *kal pa*, Skt. *yuga*) An eon that lasts in the order of millions of years.

Karma. (Tib. *lay*) Literally "action." The unerring law of cause and effect, eg. Positive actions bring happiness and negative actions bring suffering. The actions of each sentient being are the causes that create the conditions for rebirth and the circumstances in that lifetime.

Karma Kagyu. (Tib.) One of the eight schools of the Kagyu lineage of Tibetan Buddhism which is headed by His Holiness Karmapa.

Karmapa. The name means Buddha activities. The Karmapas are the head of the Kagyu school of Buddhism and were the first to implement the tradition of incarnate lamas. Karmapas are thought to be an emanation of the bodhisattva Avalokiteshvara.

Kayas, three. (Tib. *ku sum*) There are three bodies of the Buddha: the nirmanakaya, sambhogakaya and dharmakaya. The dharmakaya, also called the "truth body," is the complete enlightenment or the complete wisdom of the Buddha that is unoriginated wisdom beyond form and manifests in the sambhogakaya and the nirmanakaya. The sambhogakaya, also called the "enjoyment body," manifests only to bodhisattvas. The nirmanakaya, also called the "emanation body," manifests in the world and in this context manifests as the Shakyamuni Buddha. The fourth kaya is the svabhavakakaya which the "essence body" and the unity of the other three.

King Indrabhuti. An Indian king during the time of the Buddha who become an accomplished master. He symbolizes the person of the highest calibre who can use sense pleasures as the path of practice.

Klesha. (Tib. *nyön mong*) Also called the "disturbing emotions," these are the emotional afflictions or obscurations (in contrast to intellectual obscurations) that disturb the clarity of perception. These are also translated as "poisons." They include any emotion that disturbs or distorts consciousness. The three main kleshas are desire, anger and ignorance. The five kleshas are the three above plus pride and envy/jealousy.

Lama. (Skt. *guru*) *La* nobody above himself or herself in spiritual experience and *ma* expressing compassion like a mother. Thus the union of wisdom and compassion, feminine and masculine qualities. Lama is also a title given to a practitioner who has completed some extended training.

Liberation. (see *enlightenment*)

Lower realm. The three lower realms are birth as a hell being, hungry ghost and animal.

Luminosity. (Tib. *selwa*) In the third turning of the wheel of dharma, the Buddha taught that everything is void, but this voidness is not completely empty because it has luminosity. Luminosity or clarity allows all phenomena to appear and is a characteristic of and inseparable from emptiness (Skt. *shunyata*). Luminosity is also often used for the Tibetan word *osel*, which literally means "free from the darkness of unknowing and endowed with the ability to cognize." The two aspects are "empty luminosity," like a clear open sky; and "manifest luminosity," such as colored light images, and so forth. Luminosity is the uncompounded nature present throughout all of samsara and nirvana.

Madhyamaka. (Tib. *u ma*) The most influential of the four schools of Indian Buddhism founded by Nagarjuna in the second century C.E. The name comes from the Sanskrit word meaning "the Middle-way" meaning it is the middle way between eternalism and nihilism. The main postulate of this school is that all phenomena – both internal mental events and external physical objects – are empty of any true nature. The school uses extensive rational reasoning to establish the emptiness of phenomena. This school does, however, hold that phenomena do exist on the conventional or relative level of reality.

Mahamudra. (Tib. *cha ja chen po*) Literally means "great seal" or "great symbol" meaning that all phenomena are sealed by the primordially perfect true nature. This form of meditation is traced back to Saraha (10th century) and was passed down in the Kagyu school through Marpa. This meditative transmission emphasizes perceiving mind directly rather than through rational analysis. It also refers to the experience of the practitioner where one attains the union of emptiness and luminosity and also perceives the non-duality of the phenomenal world and emptiness; also the name of Kagyupa lineage.

Mahapandita. (Tib. *pan di ta chen po*) *Maha* means great and *pandita* Buddhist scholar.

Mahasiddha. (Tib. *drup thop chen po*) A practitioner who has a great deal of realization. *Maha* means great and *siddha* refers to an accomplished practitioner. These were particularly vajrayana practitioners who lived in India between the eight and twelfth century and practiced tantra. The biography of some of the most famous is found in *The Eighty-four Mahasiddhas.*

Mahayana. (Tib. *tek pa chen po*) Literally, the "Great Vehicle." These are the teachings of the second turning of the wheel of dharma, which emphasize shunyata (see *shunyata*), compassion and universal buddha nature. The purpose of enlightenment is to liberate all sentient beings from suffering as well as oneself. Mahayana schools of philosophy appeared several hundred years after the Buddha's death, although the tradition is traced to a teaching he is said to have given at Rajgriha, or Vulture Peak Mountain.

Mandala. (Tib. *chil kor*) Literally "centre and surrounding" but has different contexts. A diagram used in various Vajrayana practices that usually has a central deity and four directions.

Manjushri. One of the eight bodhisattvas. He is the personification of transcendent knowledge.

Mantra. (Tib. *ngags*) 1) A synonym for Vajrayana. 2) A particular combination of sounds symbolizing the nature of a deity, for example OM MANI PEME HUNG (Tib. *ngak*). These are invocations to various meditation deities which are recited in Sanskrit. These Sanskrit syllables, representing various energies, are repeated in different vajrayana practices.

Mantra vehicle. Another term for the vajrayana.

Mara. (Tib. *du*) Difficulties encountered by the practitioner. The Tibetan word means heavy or thick. In Buddhism mara symbolizes the passions

Glossary of Terms

that overwhelm human beings as well as everything that hinders the arising of wholesome roots and progress on the path to enlightenment. There are four kinds: *skandha-mara,* which is incorrect view of self; *klesha-mara,* which is being overpowered by negative emotions; *matyu-mara,* which is death and interrupts spiritual practice; and *devaputra-mara,* which is becoming stuck in the bliss that comes from meditation.

Marpa. (1012-1097 C.E.) Marpa was known for being a Tibetan who made three trips to India and brought back many tantric texts, including the Six Yogas of Naropa, the Guhyasamaja, and the Chakrasamvara practices. His root teacher was Tilopa, the founder of the Kagyu lineage and the teacher of Naropa. Marpa initiated and founded the Kagyu lineage in Tibet.

Mental consciousness. (Tib. *yid kyi namshe*) The sixth consciousness is the faculty of thinking which produces thoughts based upon the experiences of the five sense consciousnesses or its own previous content. (see *eight consciousnesses*).

Mental factors. (Tib. *sem yung*) Mental factors are contrasted to mind in that they are more long-term propensities of mind including eleven virtuous factors such as faith, detachment, and equanimity, and the six root defilements such as desire, anger, and pride, and the twenty secondary defilements such as resentment, dishonesty, harmfulness.

Middle-way. (Tib. *u ma*) or Madhyamaka school. A philosophical school founded by Nagarjuna and based on the Prajnaparamita sutras of emptiness.

Milarepa. (1040-1123 C.E.) Milarepa was a student of Marpa who attained enlightenment in one lifetime. *Mila,* named by the deities and *repa* means white cotton. His student Gampopa established the (*Dagpo*) Kagyu lineage in Tibet.

Mind-only school. Also called Cittamatra school. This is one of the major schools in the mahayana tradition founded in the fourth century by Asanga that emphasized everything is mental events.

Mother tantra. (Tib. *ma gyu*) There are three kinds tantras: *the father tantra,* which is concerned with transforming aggression; the *mother tantra,* which is concerned with transforming passion and the non-dual tantra, which concerns transforming ignorance.

Mudra. (Tib. *chak gya*) In this book it is a "hand seal" or gesture that is performed in specific tantric rituals to symbolize certain aspects of the practice being done. Also can mean spiritual consort, or the "bodily form" of a deity.

Nadi. The channels in the vajra body through which the winds flow.

Naga. (Tib. *lu*) A water spirit which may take the form of a serpent. It is often the custodian of treasures either texts or actual material treasures under ground.

Nagarjuna. (Tib. *ludrup)* An Indian master of philosophy. Founder of the Madhyamaka school and author of the *Mula-prajna* and other important works. (2nd - 3rd century)

Nalanda. The greatest Buddhist University from the fifth to the 10th century located near modern Rajgir which was the seat of the Mahayana teachings and had many great Buddhist scholars who studied there.

Naropa. (956-1040 C.E.) An Indian master best known for transmitting many Vajrayana teachings to Marpa who took these back to Tibet before the Moslem invasion of India.

Ngöndro. Tibetan for preliminary practice. One usually begins the vajrayana path by doing the four preliminary practices which involve about 111,000 refuge prayers and prostrations, 111,000 Vajrasattva mantras, 111,000 mandala offerings, and 111,000 guru yoga practices.

Nihilism. (Tib. *chad lta*) Literally, "the view of discontinuance." The extreme view of nothingness: no rebirth or karmic effects, and the non-existence of a mind after death.

Nirmanakaya. (Tib. *tulku*) There are three bodies of the Buddha and the nirmanakaya or "emanation body" manifests in the world and in this context manifests as the Shakyamuni Buddha. (see *kayas, three.)*

Nirvana. (Tib. *nyangde*) Literally, "extinguished." Individuals live in samsara and with spiritual practice can attain a state of enlightenment in which all false ideas and conflicting emotions have been extinguished. This is called nirvana. The nirvana of a Hinayana practitioner is freedom from cyclic existence, an arhat. The nirvana of a Mahayana practitioner is buddhahood, free from extremes of dwelling in either samsara or the perfect peace of an arhat.

Nondistraction. (Tib. *yengs med*) Not straying from the continuity of the practice.

Nonfabrication. (Tib. *zo med*) The important key point in meditation of Mahamudra and Dzogchen; that inate wakefulness is not created through intellectual effort.

Nonmeditation. (Tib. *gom med*) The state of not holding on to an object

Glossary of Terms

meditated upon nor a subject who meditates. Also refers to the fourth stage of Mahamudra in which nothing further needs to be meditated upon or cultivated.

Nonthought. (Tib. *mi tog*) A state in which conceptual thinking is absent.

Nyingma. (Tib.) The oldest school of Buddhism based on the teachings of Padmasambhava and others in the eighth and ninth centuries.

Obscurations. There are two categories of obscurations or defilements that cover one's Buddha-essence: the defilement of mental afflictions (see *kleshas*) and the defilement of latent tendencies or sometimes called the obscuration of dualistic perception, or the obscuration of the knowable. The first category prevents sentient beings from freeing themselves from samsara (liberation), while the second prevents them from gaining accurate knowledge and realising truth (omniscience/Buddhahood).

Occurrence. (Tib. *gyu ba*) The period when thoughts are arising in the mind. Compare with "stillness."

One-pointedness. (Tib. *Tse cig*) The first stage in the practice of Mahamudra.

One taste, (Tib. *ro cig*) The third stage in the practice of Mahamudra.

Oral instructions. (Tib. *man ngag, dams ngag*) As opposed to the scholastic traditions, the oral instructions of the Practice lineages are concise and pithy so they can always be kept in ind; they are practical and to the point so they are effective means to deal directly with the practice.

Padmasambhava. (Tib. *Guru Rinpoche*) Or the "Lotus Born." The great 8th century Indian mahasiddha who came to Tibet taming all the negative elemental forces and spreading the Buddhadharma. In particular he taught many tantras and Vajrayana practices, and concealed many texts to be later revealed by his disciples.

Pandita. A great scholar.

Paramita. "Transcendental" or "Perfection." Pure actions free from dualistic concepts that liberate sentient beings from samsara. The six paramitas are: diligence, patience, morality, generosity, contemplation, and transcendental knowledge or insight.

Path of Liberation. (Tib. *drol lam*) The path of Mahamudra practice.

Path of Means. (Tib. *thab lam*) Refers to the Six Yogas of Naropa as well as to the stages of creation and completion with attributes.

Partial compassion. The desire to feel sorry for and want to help others, but only if they are of a certain gender, race, ethnic group, social status, etc.

Paranirvana. After the Buddha Shakyamuni passed from this realm: Buddhas are not said to have died, since they have reached the stage of deathlessness, or deathless awareness.

Phowa. (Tib.) There are different kinds of phowa practice. The highest result of *dharmakaya phowa* and *sambhogakaya phowa* is full enlightenment. In this text, reference has primarily been to *nirmanakaya phowa*, called "the phowa that one practices" and to *Kacho Phowa*, an advanced tantric practice of dream yoga and clear light yoga concerned with the ejection of consciousness at death to a favourable realm or rebirth.

Pointing-out instructions. (Tib. *ngo sprod kyi gdampa*) The direct introduction to the nature of mind.

Prana. Life supporting energy. The "winds" or energy-currents of the vajra body.

Prajna. (Tib. *she rab*) In Sanskrit it means "perfect knowledge" and can mean wisdom, understanding or discrimination. Usually it means the wisdom of seeing things from a high (e.g. non-dualistic) point of view.

Prajnaparamita. (Tib. *she rab chi parol tu chinpa*) Transcendent perfect knowledge. The Tibetan literally means, "gone to the other side" or "gone beyond" as expressed in the prajnaparamita mantra, "Om gate gate paragate parasamgate bodhi svaha." The realization of emptiness in the Prajnaparamita Hridaya or Heart Sutra made possible by the extraordinarily profound dharma of the birth of Shakyamuni Buddha in the world and the practices that came from it, such as the Vajrayana tantras, which make use of visualization and the control of subtle physical energies.

Prajnaparamita sutras. Used to refer to a collection of about 40 Mahayana sutras that all deal with the realization of prajna.

Prasangika school, or Consequence School. The Rangtong middle way has two main schools, the Svatantrika and the Prasangika. The tradition comes down from Buddhapalita (his commentary on Nagarjuna) and then Chandrakirti and is the tradition of not asserting anything about the nature of genuine reality, because reality is beyond conceptual fabrication.

Pratyekabuddha. "Solitary Awakened One." These are the body disciples of the Buddha. One who has attained awakening for himself, and on his own, with no teacher in that life. Generally placed on a level between arhat and Buddha. It is the fruition of the second level of the Hinayana path through contemplation on the twelve interdependent links in reverse order.

Preta. (Tib. *yid dvags*) Hungry ghost. One of the six classes of sentient beings. Such beings are tormented by their own impure karmic perception causing them to suffer tremendously from craving, hunger and thirst. It is said that even if they came upon a lake of pure fresh water, due to their heavy karmic obscurations, they would see it as an undrinkable pool of pus. Pretas are depicted with very large bodies and very thin necks.

Provisional meaning. The teachings of the Buddha which have been simplified or modified to the capabilities of the audience. This contrasts with the definitive meaning.

Rangjung Dorje. (1284-1339 C.E.) The Third Karmapa, especially well known for writing a series of texts widely used in the Kagyu school.

Rangtong school. The Madhyamaka or Middle-way is divided into two major schools; Rangtong (empty of self) and Shentong (empty of other). Rangtong is from the second turning of the wheel of dharma and teaches reality is empty of self and beyond concepts.

Rebirth. Continuous, cyclic rebirth into the realm of samsara. Consciousness of an individual enters form according to his or her karma, the causes and conditions created by previous actions.

Recognition. (Tib. *ngo shes, ngo phrod*) In this context it means "recognizing the nature of mind."

Root guru. (Tib. *tsa way lama*) A practitioner of Vajrayana can have several types of root guru: the vajra master who confers empowerment, who bestows reading transmission, or who explains the meaning of the tantras. The ultimate root guru is the master who gives the "pointing out instructions" so that one recognizes the nature of mind.

Sacred outlook. (Tib. *dag snang*) Awareness and compassion lead the practitioner to experience emptiness (*shunyata*). From that comes luminosity manifesting as the purity and sacredness of the phenomenal world. Since the sacredness comes out of the experience of emptiness, the absence of preconceptions, it is neither a religious nor a secular vision: that is, spiritual and secular vision could meet. Moreover, sacred outlook is not conferred by any god. Seen clearly, the world is self-existingly sacred.

Sadhana. (Tib. *drup tap*) Tantric liturgy and procedure for practice, usually emphasizing the generation stage.

Samadhi. (Tib. *tin ne zin*) A state of meditation that is non-dualistic. There is an absence of discrimination between self and other. Also called meditative absorption or one-pointed meditation; this is the highest form of meditation.

Samantabhadra. *Samanta* means all and *bhadra* means excellent. "He who is All-pervadingly Good" or "He who's Beneficence is Everywhere." There are two Samantabhadras, one is the dharmakaya and the other is one of the eight main bodhisattvas, embodiment of all Buddhas aspirations. In the Vajrayana tradition Samantabhadra is the primordial Buddha and representative of the experiential content of the dharmakaya.

Samaya. (Tib. *dam sig*) The vows or commitments made in the Vajrayana to a teacher or to a practice. Many details exist but essentially it consists of outwardly, maintaining a harmonious relationship with the vajra master and one's dharma friends and inwardly, not straying from the continuity of the practice.

Sambhogakaya. (Tib. *long chö dzok ku*) There are three bodies of the Buddha and the sambhogakaya, also called the "enjoyment body," is a realm of the dharmakaya that only manifests to bodhisattvas (see *kayas, three*).

Samsara. (Tib. *kor wa*) "Cyclic existence." The conditioned existence of ordinary life in which suffering occurs because one still possesses attachment, aggression and ignorance. It is contrasted to nirvana. Through the force of karma motivated by ignorance, desire and anger one is forced to take on the impure aggregates and circle the wheel of existence until liberation.

Sangha. (Tib. *gen dun*) "Virtuous One." *Sang* means intention or motivation and *gha* means virtuous. One with virtuous motivation. One of the three jewels. Generally refers to the followers of Buddhism, and more specifically to the community of monks and nuns. The exalted sangha is those who have attained a certain level of realization of the Buddha's teachings.

Saraha. (*circa* 9th century) One of the eighty-four mahasiddhas of India who was known for his spiritual songs about Mahamudra.

Sautrantika school or Sutra school. One of the four major schools of Indian Buddhism and one of the two main hinayana schools. This school has further subschools, but basically it's view is that relative truth refers to what has only general characteristics, eg., the objects of our thoughts such as when we think fire (this appears as a concept to our mind and not the five senses), and ultimate truth is that which has specific characteristics and can perform a function such as a specific instance of fire which appears to the senses and can actually burn. In terms of general perception we mix these two together.

Selflessness. (Tib. *dag me*) Also called egolessness. In two of the hinayana schools (Vaibhashika and Sautrantika) this referred exclusively to the fact that "a person" is not a real permanent self, but rather just a collection of thoughts and feelings. In two of the mahayana schools (Cittamatra and

Madhyamaka) this was extended to mean there was no inherent existence to outside phenomena as well.

Selflessness of person. (Skt. *pudgalanairatmya*) This doctrine asserts that when one examines or looks for the person, one finds that it is empty and without self. The person does not possess a self (Skt. *atman*, Tib. *bdag-nyid*) as an independent or substantial self. This position is held by most Buddhist schools.

Selflessness of phenomena. (Skt. *dharma-nairatmya*) This doctrine asserts than not only is there selflessness of the person, but when one examines outer phenomena, one finds that external phenomena are also empty, i.e. it does not have an independent or substantial nature. This position is not held by the hinayana schools, but is put forth by the mahayana schools, particularly the Cittamatra school.

Sentient beings. With consciousness, an animated being as opposed to an inanimate object. All beings with consciousness or mind who have not attained the liberation of buddhahood. This includes those individuals caught in the sufferings of samsara as well as those who have attained the levels of a bodhisattva.

Seven dharmas of Vairochana. These are the main positions of posture for meditation: (1) Straighten the upper body and the spinal column, (2) Look slightly downward into space straight across from the tip of the nose while keeping the chin and neck straight, (3) Straighten the shoulder blades in the manner of a vulture flexing its wings, (4) Keep the lips touching gently, (5) Let the tip of the tongue touch the upper palate, (6) Form the legs into either the lotus (Skt. *padmasana*) or the diamond (Skt. *vajrasana*) posture, and (7) Keep the back of the right hand flat on the left open palm with the inside of the tips of the thumbs gently touching.

Shamatha. (Tib.) See tranquillity meditation.

Shamatha with support. (Tib. *shinay ten cas*) The practice of calming the mind while using an object of concentration, material or mental, or simply the breath.

Shamatha without support. (Tib. *shinay ten med*) The act of calming the mind without any particular object, resting undistractedly. This practice serves as a prelude for Mahamudra and should not be mistaken for the ultimate result.

Shantideva. A great bodhisattva of classical India, author of the *Bodhicharyavatara: The Guide to the Bodhisattva's Way of Life.* - (late 7th century - mid 8th century CE.)

Shastra. (Tib. *tan chö*) The Buddhist teachings are divided into words of the Buddha (the *sutras*) and the commentaries of others on his works the (*shastras*).

Shentong school. The Madhyamaka or Middle-way is divided into two major schools; Rangtong (empty of self) and Shentong (empty of other). Shentong is from the third turning of the wheel of dharma and explains ultimate reality is emptiness and luminosity inseparable.

Shravaka. "Hearer" corresponds to the level of arhat, those that seek and attain liberation for oneself through listening to the Buddhas teaching and gaining insight into selflessness and the four truths. These are the Buddhas speech disciples.

Siddha. (Tib. *drup top*) An accomplished Buddhist practitioner.

Siddhi. (Tib. *ngodrup*) "Accomplishment." The spiritual accomplishments of accomplished practitioners. Usually refers to the "supreme siddhi" of complete enlightenment, but can also mean the "common siddhis," eight mundane accomplishments.

Simplicity. (Tib. *spros ral*) 1) The absence of creating mental constructs or conceptual formations about the nature of things. 2) The second stage in the practice of Mahamudra.

Six consciousnesses. The five sensory consciousnesses and the mental consciousness.

Six realms. The realms of the six classes of beings: gods, demigods, humans, animals, hungry ghosts and hell beings.

Six Yogas of Naropa. (Tib. *naro chödruk*) These six special yogic practices were transmitted from Naropa to Marpa and consist of the subtle heat practice, the illusory body practice, the dream yoga practice, the luminosity practice, the ejection of consciousness practice and the bardo practice.

Skandha. (Tib. *pung pa*) Literally "heaps." These are the five basic transformations that perceptions undergo when an object is perceived: form, feeling, perception, formation and consciousness. First is form, which includes all sounds, smells, etc.; everything we usually think of as outside the mind. The second and third are sensations (pleasant and unpleasant, etc.) and their identification. Fourth is mental events, which include the second and third aggregates. The fifth is ordinary consciousness, such as the sensory and mental consciousnesses.

Skilful means. (Tib. *thabs*) Ingenuity in application. Generally, upaya conveys the sense that enlightened beings teach the dharma skilfully, taking into consideration the various needs, abilities, and shortcomings of their

Glossary of Terms

students. Upaya is an expression of compassion. In the bodhisattva's discipline, it corresponds to the first five paramitas and to relative bodhicitta. By prajna alone, without upaya, the bodhisattva is fettered to a quietistic nirvana. By upaya without prajna, one remains bound to samsara. Therefore the practitioner must unify them.

In Vajrayana, upaya arises from shunyata. It is joined with prajna and represents the male, form aspect of the union of form and emptiness.

Spiritual song. (Skt. *doha*, Tib. *gur*) A religious song spontaneously composed by a Vajrayana practitioner. It usually has nine syllables per line.

Stillness. (Tib. *gnas pa*) Absence of thought activity and disturbing emotions, but with subtle fixation on this stillness.

Subtle channels. (Skt. *nadi*, Tib. *tsa*) These refer to the subtle channels which are not anatomical ones but ones in which psychic energies or "winds" (Skt. *prana*, Tib. *lung*) travel.

Suchness. See dharmata.

Supreme siddhi. Another word for enlightenment.

Sutra. (Tib. *do*) Literally "Junction." The combination of the Hinayana and Mahayana, or the combination of wisdom and compassion. Texts in the Buddhist cannon attributed to the Buddha. They are viewed as his recorded words, although they were not actually written down until many years after his *paranirvana*. They are usually in the form of dialogues between the Buddha and his disciples. These are often contrasted with the tantras which are the Buddha's Vajrayana teachings and the shastras which are commentaries on the words of the Buddha.

Sutra Mahamudra. (Tib. *mdo'i phyag chen*) The Mahamudra system based on the Prajnaparamita scriptures and emphasizing Shamatha and Vipashyana and the progressive journey through the five paths and ten bhumis.

Sutrayana. The sutra approach to achieving enlightenment which includes the Hinayana and the Mahayana.

Svatantrika or *Autonomy School.* The reason why this school is called the autonomy school is that they assert the autonomous existence of valid reasons that prove their point. The Rangtong middle way has two main schools, the Svatantrika and the Prasangika. The Svatantrika has two main sub-schools which both assert conventional reality to be like illusions, but do so according to either the sutra school or the Mind-only school. Ultimate reality it asserts is emptiness and free from conceptual fabrication.

Svabhavakakaya. (Tib. *ngo bo nyid kyi sku*) The "essence body." Sometimes counted as the fourth kaya, the unity of the first three.

Tantra. (Tib. *gyu.*) Literally, tantra means "continuity," and in Buddhism it refers to two specific things: the texts (resultant texts, or those that take the result as the path) that describe the practices leading from ignorance to enlightenment, including commentaries by tantric masters; and the way to enlightenment itself, encompassing the ground, path, and fruition. One can divide Buddhism into the sutra tradition and the tantra tradition. The sutra tradition primarily involves the academic study of the Mahayana sutras and the tantric path primarily involves practicing the Vajrayana practices. The tantras are primarily the texts of the Vajrayana practices.

Tantra Mahamudra (Tib. *sngags kyi phyag chen*) The same as mantra Mahamudra. The Mahamudra practice connected to the six dharmas of Naropa.

Tathagatagarbha. The same as Buddha-essence. The inherently present potential for enlightenment in all sentient beings.

Ten non-virtuous actions. Killing, stealing, sexual misconduct, lying, slander, abusive words, idle gossip, covetousness, ill-will, and wrong views. Acts are non-virtuous or unwholesome when they result in undesirable karmic effects. Thus, this list of ten unwholesome acts occurs generally in discussions of the functioning of karma. The first three are actions of body, the next four of speech, and the last three of mind. The ten virtuous actions are the opposites of the above ten non-virtuous actions.

Ten stages. The stages or bodhisattva levels in the Mahayana path which are: 1) The Joyous One with an emphasis on generosity, 2) The Stainless One with an emphasis on discipline, 3) The Illuminating One with an emphasis on patience, 4) The Flaming One with an emphasis on exertion, 5) The One Difficult to Conquer with an emphasis on samadhi, 6) The Manifest One with an emphasis on wisdom, 7) The Far Going One with an emphasis on skilful activity, 8) The Unshakeable One with an emphasis on future, 9) The One of Good Discrimination with an emphasis on efficacy, 10) Cloud of Dharma with an emphasis on accomplishing enlightenment. In the tantric (Vajrayana) literature there are three more stages of manifesting enlightenment, making thirteen in total.

Tenjur. Commentary on the Kanjur; also tantras of meditation, healing, scientific and technical instructions etc.

Therevada. (Tib. *neten depa*) A school, sometimes called the Hinayana, which is the foundation of Buddhism and this school emphasizes the careful examination of mind and its confusion.

Three jewels. (Tib. *kön chok sum*) Literally "three precious ones." The three essential components of Buddhism: Buddha, dharma, sangha, i.e., the Awakened One, the truth expounded by him, and the followers living in accordance with this truth. Firm faith in the three precious ones is the stage of "stream entry." The three precious ones are objects of veneration and are considered "places of refuge." The Buddhist takes refuge by pronouncing the threefold refuge formula, thus acknowledging formally to be a Buddhist.

Three realms. These are three categories of samsara. The desire realm includes existences where beings are reborn with solid bodies due to their karma ranging from the deva paradises to the hell realms. The form realm is where beings are reborn due to the power of meditation; and their bodies are of subtle form in this realm. These are the meditation paradises. The formless realm is where beings due to their meditation (samadhi), have entered a state of meditation after death and the processes of thought and perception have ceased.

Three roots. Guru, yidam and dakini. Guru is the root of blessings, yidam of accomplishment and dakini of activity.

Three sufferings. These are the suffering of suffering, the suffering of change, and pervasive suffering (meaning the inherent suffering in all of samsara).

Three vehicles. Hinayana, Mahayana and Vajrayana.

Tilopa. (928-1009 C.E.) One of the eighty-four mahasiddhas who became the guru of Naropa who transmitted his teachings to the Kagyu lineage in Tibet.

Tögal. (Tib.) "Leap over," "direct crossing" or "passing above." Dzogchen has two main sections: Trekcho and Tögal. The former emphasizes primordial purity and the latter spontaneous presence.

Traces of actions. (Skt. *vasana.* Tib. *bakchak*) Patterns of conditional response that exist as traces or tendencies stored in the alaya-vijnana, the eigthh consciousness sometimes called the store-house or all-base consciousness. So called because it is a repository of all karmically conditioned patterns. All dualistic or ego-oriented experiences leave a residue, which is stored in the alaya-vijnana until a later time when some conscious occurrence activates the habitual pattern. The pattern then generates a response in the form of a perception or an action. This response leaves its own karmic residue, stored again in the unconscious repository, and the cycle continues. The explanation of this system is a central teaching of the Cittamatrin tradition of Mahayana Buddhism.

Tranquillity meditation. (Tib. *shinay*, Skt. *Shamatha*) One of the two main types of meditation, calm abiding, the meditative practice of calming the mind in order to rest free from the disturbance of thought activity, the other is insight.

Tummo. (Tib.) An advanced Vajrayana practice for combining bliss and emptiness which produces heat as a by product. This is one of the Six Yogas of Naropa.

Two accumulations. (Tib. *shogs nyis*) The accumulation of merit with concepts and the accumulation of wisdom beyond concepts.

Two truths. Conventional truth and absolute truth. Relative truth describes the superficial and apparent mode of all things. Ultimate truth describes the true and unmistaken mode of all things. These two are described differently in the different schools, each progressively deeper leading closer to the way things are.

Vaibhashika school. One of the four major schools of Indian Buddhism and one of the two major Hinayana schools. Sometimes translated as the Particularist school. It defines relative truth as whatever can be broken down into parts and ultimate truth as that which cannot be broken down, eg, indivisible atoms and moments of consciousness.

Vairochana. (Tib. *nam par nang dze*) The sambhogakaya Buddha of the Buddha family.

Vajra. (Tib. *dorje*) Usually translated "diamond like." This may be an implement held in the hand during certain Vajrayana ceremonies, or it can refer to a quality which is so pure and so enduring that it is like a diamond.

Vajra posture. This refers to the full-lotus posture in which the legs are interlocked. When one leg is placed before the other as many Westerners sit it is called the half-lotus posture.

Vajradhara. (Tib. *Dorje Chang*) "Holder of the vajra." *Vajra* means indestructible and *dhara* means holding, embracing or inseparable. The central figure in the Kagyu refuge tree, and indicating the transmission of the close lineage of the Mahamudra teachings to Tilopa. Vajradhara symbolizes the primordial wisdom of the dharmakaya and wears the ornaments of the sambhogakaya Buddha, symbolizing its richness.

Vajrasattva. (Tib. *Dorje Sempa*) The Buddha of purification. Vajrasattva practice is part of the four preliminary practices. A sambhogakaya Buddha who embodies all the five families. He is also a major source of purification practices.

Vajrayogini. (Tib. *Dorje Palmo*) A semi-wrathful yidam. Female.

Vajrayana. (Tib. *dorje tek pa*) Literally, "diamond-like" or "indestructible capacity." *Vajra* here refers to method, so you can say the method yana. There are three major traditions of Buddhism (Hinayana, Mahayana, Vajrayana) The Vajrayana is based on the tantras and emphasizes the clarity aspect of phenomena. A practitioner of the method of taking the result as the path.

Vase breathing. (Tib. *bum can gyi lung byor*) An advanced breathing practice which has to be learned under the supervision of an experienced teacher and involves the retention of the breath in the abdomen which is thus like an air filled vase.

Vasubandhu. (4th Century C.E.) A great fourth century Indian scholar who was brother of Asanga and wrote the Hinayana work the *Abhidharmakosha* explaining the Abhidharma.

Vidyadhara. Holder of knowledge or insight: the energy of discovery and communication. An accomplished master of the Vajrayana teachings.

View, meditation, and conduct. (Tib. *ta ba gom pa yodpa*) The philosophical orientation, the act of growing accustomed to that – usually in sitting practice, and the implementation of that insight during the activities of daily life. Each of the three vehicles has its particular definition of view, meditation and action.

Vinaya. One of the three major sections of the Buddha's teachings showing ethics, what to avoid and what to adopt. The other two sections are the sutras and the abhidharma.

Vipashyana meditation. (Tib. *lha tong*) Sanskrit for "insight meditation." This meditation develops insight into the nature of reality (Skt. *dharmata*). One of the two main aspects of meditation practice, the other being Shamatha.

Wheel of dharma. (Skt. *dharmachakra*) The Buddha's teachings correspond to three levels which very briefly are: the first turning was the teachings on the four noble truths and the teaching of the egolessness of person; the second turning was the teachings on emptiness and the emptiness of phenomena; the third turning was the teachings on luminosity and buddha nature.

Whispered lineage. (Tib. *nyan gyu*) A lineage of instruction passed orally from teacher to disciple. Teachings of a hearing lineage are usually very secret, since they can only be received by direct, personal communication with the guru. "Hearing lineage" is also a common epithet for the Kagyu lineage.

Yana. Means capacity. There are three yanas, narrow, (Hinayana) great (Mahayana) and indestructible (Vajrayana).

Yidam. (Tib.) *Yi* means mind and *dam* means pure, or *yi* means your mind and *dam* means inseparable. The yidam represents the practitioner's awakened nature or pure appearance. A tantric deity that embodies qualities of buddhahood and is practiced in the Vajrayana. Also called a tutelary deity.

Yidam meditation. (Tib.) Yidam meditation is the Vajrayana practice that uses the visualization of a yidam.

Yoga. "Natural condition." A person who practices this is called a *yogi,* characterized by leaving everything natural, just as it is, e.g. not washing or cutting your hair and nails etc. A female practitioner is called a *yogini*.

Yogi. (Tib *nal yor pa*) Tantric practitioner.

Yogini. (Tib *nal yor ma*) Female tantric practitioner.

Index

84,000 teachings 2, 91, 110

A

Abhidharma 56, 57, 87, 102
Abhidharmakosha 56
Absolute truth 57, 58, 69, 85, 101, 115, 119
Accumulations 3, 117, 138
    Accumulation of merit 138
Afflicted consciousness 52
Alaya consciousness 52
Alertness 113, 115
All-basis 39, 124
All-good stage 9
Amrita 12
Approximate wisdom 12
Arhat 94, 115
Arhatship 115
Aspirational Prayer of Mahamudra 51, 60, 70, 137
Attentiveness 84, 128, 134
Awareness 16, 17, 39, 40, 51, 57, 67, 86, 111, 112, 119-122, 128, 129, 132, 133
Naked awareness 121, 122, 132, 133

B

Bewilderment 112
Bhikshu 10, 11, 15
Bindu 12, 129
Blessing 6, 12, 38, 44, 75, 98, 100, 102, 111, 134, 137, 138
Bodhi tree 20
Bodhichitta 123
Bodhisattva 45, 94, 115
Bodhisattva level 115
Buddha Shakyamuni 3
Buddha-essence 16, 17, 63, 137
Buddhahood 1, 38, 90, 102, 104, 115

C

Chakra 26, 44
Chakrasamvara 3-5, 11, 13, 14, 20, 22, 24
Channels 12, 21, 67, 68, 74, 129, 131
Chittamatra 16
Chöd 73, 74
Compassion 2, 3, 5, 37, 95, 123, 137

Completion stage 4, 11, 13, 14, 44
Confidence 48, 52, 64, 69, 75, 76, 132
Confusion 57, 58, 61, 77, 79, 101, 109
Consciousness 52, 54, 65, 77
   Eight consciousness 52, 65
      Afflicted consciousness 52
      Alaya consciousness 52
      Mental consciousness 52, 54, 77
   Six consciousness 54
Conventional truth 57, 58
Creation stage 4, 11, 13, 89

D

Daka 22, 24
Dakini 10-13, 15, 19, 20, 22, 24, 35, 47, 49, 99
Deity 11
Devotion 5, 75, 76, 100, 102, 111, 134, 138
Dharmadhatu 52, 111
Dharmakaya 2, 3, 21-23
Dharmata 23, 24, 59, 70, 71, 74, 99, 103, 109, 112, 116, 119, 124
Direct experience 3, 17, 19, 23, 52, 53, 55, 58, 63, 69, 77, 79, 80, 86, 113, 119, 121, 132, 133, 136
Disturbing emotion 45, 46, 50, 56, 61, 87, 90, 95, 100, 109, 110, 119-125, 129-131, 135
   Klesha 9, 46, 73, 74, 112-114
   Mental afflictions 50, 53, 100, 111
Doha 16
Dzogchen 44, 71, 115

E

Eight consciousness 52, 65

Emanation 2, 3, 14, 19, 20, 22, 24
Empowerment 11-14, 23, 25, 26, 63, 83
Experiential guidance 120, 121

F

Faith 15, 26, 28, 29, 31, 134, 138
Father tantra 13, 14, 16
Fearlessness 9
Five paths 105
Fixation 11, 21, 59, 74, 78, 79, 82, 85, 90, 100, 103, 115, 125, 126
Four common preliminaries 102
Four thoughts 64, 102
Four empowerments 12
Four extremes 80
Four seals 79
Four uncommon preliminaries 91, 102
   Ngöndro 102, 138
Fruition tantra 11

G

Gampopa 52, 105, 108
Ganachakra 26
Gandharva 13
Gaze 40, 128, 129
Great bliss 12
Guhyasamaja 13
Guidance through words 120
Guru 15, 17, 35, 38, 45, 47, 48, 62, 75, 84, 91, 98-100, 102, 109, 111, 134, 138
   Root guru 84, 100
Guru-yoga 91, 102, 138

H

Heruka 10

Index

Hevajra 4, 5
Higher realm 89
Hinayana 10, 53, 63, 94, 111, 123

I

Ignorance 39, 60, 79, 90, 110-112, 117
Inferential analysis 52
Inferential reasoning 52, 57, 61, 63, 69, 118, 121, 136
Inferential view 103

J

Jamgon Kongtrul 133

K

Kagyu 17, 43, 108, 118, 130, 134
Kalachakra 44
Kalpa 36, 60, 110, 117
Karmamudra 40, 129
Karmapa 43, 47, 51, 60, 61, 70, 132, 137
King Indrabhuti 107
Klesha 9, 46, 73, 74, 112-114

L

Liberation 1, 3, 23, 38, 40, 50, 74, 84, 87, 89, 90, 93-95, 98-102, 105, 125, 126
Love 2, 31
Loving kindness 95, 123
Lower realm 84
Lucidity 38, 52, 59, 60, 65, 71, 72, 82, 104, 114, 121, 127, 128, 132, 134
Luminosity 13, 36, 37, 59-62, 64, 78, 110

M

Madhyamaka 16, 17, 52
  Rangtong school 16, 57, 59
  Shentong school 16, 17, 57
Mahasiddha 1-3, 9, 14, 15, 26, 29, 107
Mahayana 53, 63, 64, 78, 94, 111, 115, 123
Mandala 4, 11, 13, 17, 22, 138
Manifestation 3, 22, 23, 28, 45, 61, 65, 69, 71, 72, 74, 79, 80
Mantra 11, 12, 63, 74, 75, 83
Mara 74
Marpa 4, 11, 17, 41, 43, 63, 72, 108, 132
Mental afflictions 50, 53, 100, 111
Mental consciousness 52, 54, 77
Mental event 52
Mental formation 54
Middle-way 52, 70, 94, 115
Milarepa 48, 55, 65, 72, 73, 108
Mindfulness 56, 84, 112-115, 128, 134
Moonbeams of Mahamudra 43, 44, 134
Mother tantra 13, 14, 16

N

Nadi 12
Nagarjuna 5, 6, 7, 13, 59, 107
Naked awareness 121, 122, 132, 133
Nalanda 99
Namtar 1, 2, 19
Naropa 2-5, 17, 24, 25, 35, 41-43, 46-48, 63, 72, 99, 108, 114, 118, 122, 130, 132
Ngöndro 102, 138

Nirmanakaya 3, 21, 22
Nirvana 13, 70
Non-duality 46
Non-existence 71, 72, 87, 88, 100, 114, 126
Non-meditation 133
Non-virtuous action 58, 84, 90
Nyingma 111

O

Obscurations 3, 37, 39, 59, 60, 79, 89, 90, 91, 95, 110-112, 117, 121, 124, 134
Omniscience 90, 102
One-pointedness 133
One-taste 133
Oral instructions 33, 102

P

Padmasambhava 20
Pandita 26, 99, 120
Paramita 10, 37, 47, 59, 63, 78, 90, 94
Path of liberation 23, 74
Pith instruction 2, 3, 11, 13, 14, 16, 22-24, 26
Post-meditation 67, 68, 70, 77, 80, 93, 112, 113
Prajna 4, 40, 59, 93, 94, 114, 116, 129
Prajnaparamita 10, 47, 59, 63, 94
Prana 12, 129
Pratyekabuddha 94
Preta 109

R

Rangtong school 16, 57, 59
Relative truth 57, 84, 112, 115

Conventional truth 57, 58
Root guru 84, 100

S

Sadhana 53
Samadhi 11, 15, 20, 21, 28, 57, 87, 107, 108, 109, 127, 128, 130, 131
Samantabhadra 111
Samaya 20, 23, 24, 37, 49, 83-87, 89, 129
Samayamudra 129
Sambhogakaya 3, 21, 22
Sangha 107, 108
Saraha 59
Secret empowerment 12
Selflessness 53, 94, 111, 115
  Selflessness of person 53, 94, 111, 115
  Selflessness of phenomena 94
Sentient being 3, 17, 24
Seven dharmas of Vairochana 67, 68
Shamatha 95, 116, 120, 127
  Tranquillity meditation 52, 55, 127
Shentong school 16, 17, 57
Shravaka 94, 115
Siddha 1-3, 9, 14, 15, 26, 29, 45, 81, 107, 108, 116, 121, 128
Siddhi 12, 15, 40, 107, 108, 115, 130, 131
Simplicity 108, 133
Six consciousness 54
Six realms 109
Six Yogas of Naropa 3, 4, 130
Skandha 12
Skilful means 4
  Upaya 3, 40, 129
Spiritual song 17, 49, 50, 71

Index

Doha 16
Subtle channel 12, 21
Suchness 14, 15
Supreme siddhi 40, 107, 108, 115, 130, 131
Sutra 2, 16, 52, 59, 61, 63, 87, 94, 103
Sutra tradition 16, 59, 61

T

Tantra 3-5, 11, 13, 14, 16, 37, 44, 63, 78, 86, 87, 103
Three jewels 24
Three realms 54, 100
Three sufferings 99
Tögal 44
Torpor 105, 128, 134
Tranquillity meditation 52, 55, 127
Tummo 129

U

Ultimate level 57
Ultimate view 14
Upaya 4, 40, 129

V

Vairochana 67, 68

Vajradhara 3, 19, 23, 111, 117
Vajrasattva 91, 138
Vajrayana 5, 10, 52, 63, 78, 111, 115, 123
Vajrayogini 4, 20
Vanquishing behavior 9, 10, 11, 15
Vase empowerment 12
Victorious in all directions behavior 9, 10
View, meditation, and conduct 52
View, meditation, conduct and fruition 104, 125
Vipashyana 127
Virtuous action 58, 84, 89, 90, 98

W

Wheel of dharma 52, 59, 63, 64
   Second turning 52, 59, 63, 64
   Third turning 63, 64
Whispered lineage 20

Y

Yidam 13, 17, 23, 91
Yoga 61, 91, 102, 138
Yogi 3, 13, 15, 16, 20, 26
Yogini 3, 16, 20

181

The Buddhist Schools

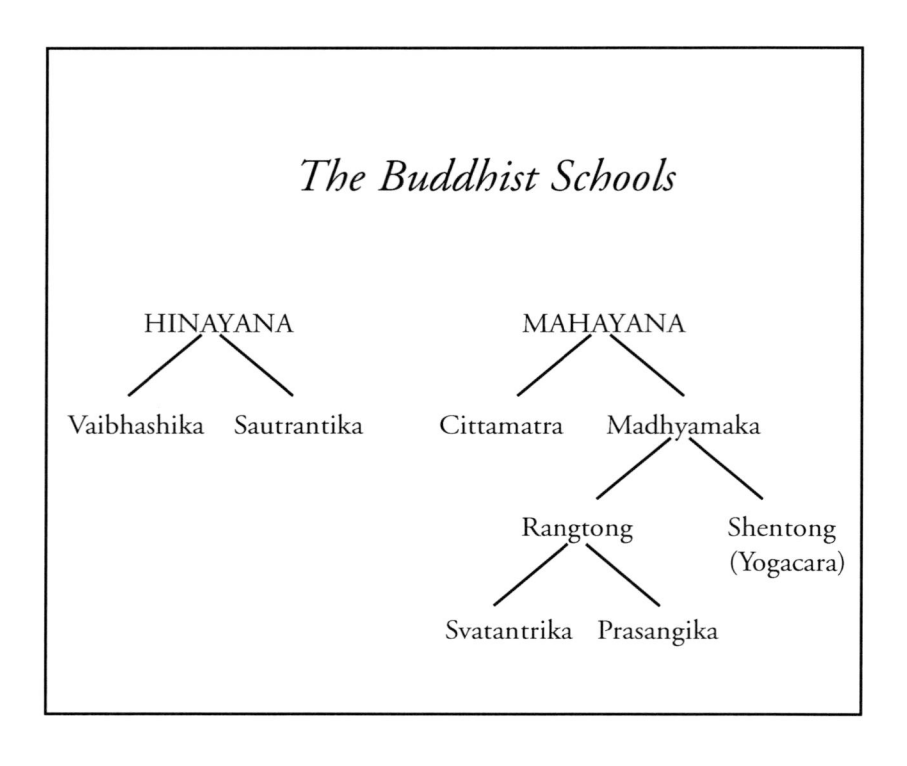

HINAYANA
- Vaibhashika
- Sautrantika

MAHAYANA
- Cittamatra
- Madhyamaka
  - Rangtong
    - Svatantrika
    - Prasangika
  - Shentong (Yogacara)

Other publications from
Zhyisil Chokyi Ghatsal

A Guide to Shamatha Meditation
Buddhist Conduct: The Ten Virtuous Actions
The Life of the Buddha & The Four Noble Truths
The Twelve Links of Interdependent Origination
Teachings on the Practice of Meditation
Four Foundations of Buddhist Practice
The Three Vehicles of Buddhist Practice
The Middle Way Meditation Instructions
Ascertaining Certainty in the View
The Two Truths
Progressive Stages of Meditation on Emptiness
Beautiful Song of Marpa the Translator
Transcending Ego: Distinguishing Consciousness from Wisdom
An Introduction to Mahamudra Meditation
An Overview of the Bardo Teachings
The Five Buddha Families and the Eight Consciousnesses
The Four Dharmas of Gampopa
Aspirational Prayer for Mahamudra
Showing the Path of Liberation
Medicine Buddha Teachings
Journey of the Mind: teachings on the bardo
The Essence of Creation & Completion
Mahamudra Teachings
The Aspiration Prayer of Mahamudra
Pointing Out the Dharmakaya
The Life of Tilopa & The Ganges Mahamudra
A Spiritual Biography of Marpa the Translator
Rechungpa, A Biography of Milarepa's Disciple

Zhyisil Chokyi Ghatsal
PO Box 6259, Wellesley St, Auckland, New Zealand
Email: orders@greatliberation.org   Website: www.greatliberation.org

Care of Dharma Books

Dharma books contain the teachings of the Buddha; they have the power to protect against lower rebirth and to point the way to Liberation. Therefore, they should be treated with respect, kept off the floor and places where people sit or walk, and not stepped over. They should be covered or protected for transporting and kept in a high, clean place separate from more "ordinary" things. If it is necessary to dispose of Dharma materials, they should be burned with care and awareness rather than thrown in the trash. When burning Dharma texts, it is considered skilful to first recite a prayer or mantra, such as OM, AH, HUNG. Then you can visualize the letters of the text (to be burned) being absorbed into the AH, and the AH being absorbed into you. After that you can burn the texts.

These considerations may be also kept in mind for Dharma artwork, as well as the written teachings and artwork of other religions.